PROBLEMS IN PSYCHOANALYSIS

A

PROBLEMS IN PSYCHOANALYSIS

A SYMPOSIUM

Marcel Raclot Charles Baudouin, Charles-Henri Nodet,
Serge Leclaire, Vladimir Granoff, Andrée Hauser,
Roland Cahen, Igor A. Caruso, A. Vergote, Paul Cossa,
Marc Oraison, Louis Beirnaert, Étienne Borne

BALTIMORE
HELICON PRESS, INC.

This translation of Problèmes de Psychanalyse
(*Librairie Arthème Fayard, Paris*) *was made by*

CECILY BATTEN

NIHIL OBSTAT: JOANNES M. T. BARTON, S.T.D., L.S.S
CENSOR DEPUTATUS
IMPRIMATUR: E. MORROGH BERNARD
VICARIUS GENERALIS
WESTMONASTER II: DIE XXVI JULII MCMLX

Library of Congress Catalog Card Number 61–8099

MADE AND PRINTED IN HOLLAND FOR HELICON PRESS, INC.
5517 SELMA AVE, BALTIMORE, 27 MD.

CONTENTS

PREFACE

This collection of articles does not profess to give a comprehensive account of the present state of Freudian thought nor to provide grounds for decisive judgement on the therapeutic, scientific or humanistic value of the analytic techniques.

Our aim is more modest. As the title indicates, we are simply concerned to throw a little light on some of the psychoanalytic problems which surround the approaches to a field which is complicated, ambiguous and difficult, where the best and the worst are often inextricably mixed. The need to discover whether Freudianism has a contribution to make towards a new humanism or whether it irreparably damages the traditional view of man underlies our undertaking, but without it being possible for us to proceed any further in the present state of affairs than to give a quite provisional answer and to indicate very tentative probabilities.

Three different kinds of contribution have made this book possible. In the first place practitioners of the analytic methods have described the sort of problem they meet and tackle in the course of their work, problems which are at the same time technical, moral and human; we have preferred serious accounts by men who are engaged in the work, even if what they write is sometimes a little heavy and slow, to the more superficial elegance of syntheses prematurely run up from outside. This is followed by an account of the various forms which analysis has taken, as the original stream of thought has not remained one and indivisible; the multiplicity of analytic trends—and we emphasize the plural—in itself constitutes a sort of objective critique of Freud's intuitions and methods. Finally the Freudian doctrine and the analytic methods are considered in relation to various spiritual and religious problems so as to explore those frontier regions where the reasons for resisting the new ideas stemming from Freud and the reasons for being open to them may be expected to be equally alive and strong.

The Freudian language has not remained within psychoanalysis, technically considered, but has flooded our civilization. Words like transference, repression and sublimation are not counters with arbitrarily determined values; a particular language is always the expression of a particular way of thought. Whether it is deplored or welcomed, Freudianism is here. Questions, then, arise of themselves—certain brusque rejections of psychoanalysis may themselves be explained psychoanalytically, and may point to an uneasy defence of a false equilibrium, but, all the same, a sound critical attitude may legitimately be disquieted at the suggestion of totalitarianism in the Freudian system. From one point of view it looks as if Freud has fallen into all the dreary earthbound heresies—positivism, scientism, determinism; from another point of view this unconscious in which time past is always to be rediscovered gives man as conceived by Freud, and perhaps man as he is in himself, a substance and a depth which could be regarded as spiritual. The techniques of psychoanalytic liberation, so easily transferable to fields other than that of mental pathology, reflect the same ambiguity; sometimes they look as if they involve a sort of violation of consciousness, forcing it to deliver up all that it regards as secret and sacred, sometimes they seem to be following the most orthodox paths of self-knowledge and the salvation of man in and by truth.

We have raised this disquiet in order to point, beyond the limits of this book, to the distant aim of our endeavour. To avoid the opportunities of attack and defence would be to condemn ourselves to illusion. Security is only too often a mistaken good which should give way to honesty. And the human spirit sometimes finds itself in a situation in which honesty consists in suffering present perplexity while remaining open and attentive to the call of some further shore, not within our immediate reach.

MEN AND TECHNIQUES

FREUD AND HIS EMPIRICAL GENIUS

EXPERIMENTAL CONDITIONS OF A TRUE DIALOGUE

Dr Marcel Raclot

Freud went to Paris as a doctor to study under Charcot, and it is hardly possible to see his work in perspective without taking this beginning into account. But he was never taken up with the wish to cure, to treat people and relieve suffering at any price; he was concerned above all with the desire to understand.

Can it be said, then, that Freud's particular genius was empirical? But is it possible to think of a genius which is not empirical, in the sense of keeping in touch with experience and reality? Reality for Freud meant in the first place the hysterical and obsessional neurotics who were under his care. But since Freud was primarily a thinker who happened also to be a doctor, the actual object of his study was just as much the psychology of the normal person as that of the mentally ill, as much 'The Psychopathology of Everyday Life' as that of temporary or permanent mental troubles.

It is, no doubt, just because his clinical analysis cannot be separated sharply and fundamentally from his analysis of the normal person, and because his medical analysis leads to a re-thinking of human psychology, that it meets with such resistance. If account is taken of the fact that he did not think of neurosis just as something which happens to the individual, but rather as something which should be thought of in terms of culture and civilization, then it is seen at once that his work, like all work of genius, illuminates some problems only to bring us up against the mystery of all the others.

Freud's work has revolutionized our understanding of the mentally ill but at the same time it never ceases to put before the normal man fresh questions which he cannot now avoid without deliberately shutting his eyes. Although psychoanalysis had its origins in the medical field it goes on to call the whole of culture in question *de facto* and *de jure*, and to disturb the mistaken presuppositions and prejudices which stand in the way of knowledge, by a method of systematic doubt as revolutionary in the affective sphere as the Cartesian doubt was in the rational sphere.

Anthropology, religion, art and sociology, while keeping to their own principles, can no longer ignore Freud's work. Freud, who continued his own self-analysis to the end of his life, never ceases to put to the normal person, as he put to his patients, the question of his own sincerity. If psychoanalysis is stripped of the over-simplified pictures and rigid concepts by which it has become constrained as an inevitable result of popularization, it is seen to follow in the direct line of a Socratic self-knowledge, although it certainly cannot be reduced to such a self-knowledge. In relation to this line of thought, it may be seen rather as a mutation, a striking out, a Copernican revolution, in that it introduces a methodological requirement that is quite new, the rule that nothing should be omitted in a dialogue between two persons, a requirement which conflicts with the inevitable omissions, the repression of everything which, in the course of his life, the patient has not been able to admit to consciousness. Self-knowledge no longer calls primarily for an effort of conscious sincerity, but rather for an attitude of receptivity towards anything which may occur to the mind.

Ill or well, man of action or thinker, philosopher, sociologist or theologian, the man who consults Freud can no longer expect to understand his own statements without taking account of all that he does not say. The one can no longer be understood without the other.

Once a man has recognized the absolute novelty of a dialogue which from the start seeks to pass beyond the self-complacency of literary autobiography and narcissism, he is led to reconsider his own deepest attitudes before the totality of human problems, and is forced to re-assess his degree of liberty, or rather, conversely, of alienation.

It was precisely this alienation, this odd way of expressing oneself, which Freud recognized in the first place in the symptoms of his neurotics. The problems raised for him by hypnosis started him off on the discovery of the analytic technique, and the difficulties resulting from induced or imposed association led him to discover the fundamental law of free association. Throughout his studies Freud never ceased to draw his concepts from experience itself and continually to modify his theory as experience required, in accordance with the method proper to scientific integrity, in which the relationship between experiment and theory is never broken in either direction.

For example, before pin-pointing the so-called Freudian pansexuality, reference should be made to the following passage, where Freud's empirical turn of mind is clearly demonstrated: 'During the study of the sexual functions it has been possible to gain a first, preliminary conviction, or rather suspicion, of two pieces of knowledge which will later be found to be important over the whole of our field. Firstly, the normal and abnormal phenomena that we observe (that is, the phenomenology of the subject) require to be described from the point of view of dynamics and of economics... And secondly, the aetiology of the disturbances which we are studying is to be found in the developmental history of the individual, that is to say, in the early part of his life.' [1]

How can a pansexual attitude be discerned in a preliminary description of normal and abnormal behaviour as observed? In the same way Freud's line of thought concerning neurosis may be seen right through its development to be

[1] *An Outline of Psychoanalysis*, Hogarth Press, 1949, p. 15.

founded on experience, modifying itself as required by new facts, and leading to a general view which Freud was ready, right to the end, to call in question.

He can no longer be seen as giving a purely historical or genetic account of neurosis. Even the hypothesis of somatic compliance is not just a routine formula and he is seen to be always attentive to the quantitative aspect of libidinal energy and to its conditioning by the endocrine glands. He even mentions the possibility of a future therapeutic approach by means of 'hormones or similar substances'. To read his books is to be constantly reminded of the scholar seeking to throw light on some phenomenon or other and mistrusting ill-founded explanations. In our view there is no doubt that this is why Freud's work so effectively illuminates human psychology, normal and pathological, within its own methodological framework.

Freud himself believed that his work threw light on normal psychology as well as abnormal, saying that neuroses 'shade off into what is described as the normal by a series of transitional steps' and that 'on the other hand there is scarcely any condition generally recognized as normal in which it would not be possible to demonstrate neurotic traits.'[1] This is just what makes the limits of the contribution which psychoanalysis has to make in the field of culture so indefinable. But Freud recognized values in themselves as being beyond the reach of psychoanalytic investigation, and since he himself had not the necessary philosophical training, he left open a dialogue which is doubtless even now far from having reached its true dimensions. If Freud has answered certain questions raised by art and religion, these in their turn are far from having answered the questions Freud has put to them.

The psychiatrist, who is surely in a better position than is sometimes thought to distinguish between normal persons, neurotics and the insane (at least if he may be credited with not always succumbing to an incapacitating institutional

[1] *Ibid.*, p. 49.

maladjustment) will pay attention not only to that which distinguishes them one from the other but also to that which they have in common, we mean the inevitable gaps in their life history, which are apparent even in the normal subject in the difficulty he has to see and describe himself. And so psychoanalysis, which started in the experimental study of the classic neuroses, is today concerned with a renewal of normal psychology, with the character neuroses and the neurotic traits in normal character. In short, as Dr Pasche has recently written: 'Psychoanalysis, without being a humanism, since it does not have to take account of values, is nevertheless the necessary introduction to true modern humanism.' This is also to give psychoanalysis a new place in psychiatry, not only as a therapeutic technique for dealing with neuroses, but also as an introduction to the whole question of the relationship between doctor and patient. As part of his training the psychiatrist learns to assess the disturbances to which his own fundamental attitudes will give rise if he is not aware of them and if he is not very careful, since one unconscious can affect another unconscious, just as much in the case of more or less minor troubles, which can be relieved by comparatively short and less systematic courses of psychotherapy, as in that of the serious psychoses regarded up to now as inaccessible.

But perhaps nothing shows us more clearly how Freud was in contact with reality—a reality which paradoxically consisted in the unconscious flight of his patients from reality—than his attitude towards the psychoses. He certainly recognized the powerlessness of psychoanalysis in face of psychosis but at the same time maintained an attitude of reserve towards other methods of approach which owe something to psychoanalysis, in that they make use of psychoanalytic knowledge concerning the conflicts of the mentally ill and their origins: despite the uncertainty caused by the somatic element in the psychoses, his psychotherapeutic approach, though far removed from the psychoanalytic couch, is unthinkable without a constant recourse to Freudian concepts. Neither individual psychotherapy, nor group psychotherapy such as psychodrama, can be thought of without reference to the Freudian unconscious. The most alienated patient is no longer 'under the doctor' but is basically a partner, with whom, through his raving distortions, a dialogue may be engaged in. This is to say also that the psychiatrist regards himself as invited, even in the case of an insane person, to recognize and master his fear, his aggressiveness, and his narcissism, obstacles which will remain insurmountable so long as they remain unconscious.

More, he is constrained to invite society to do the same, at least that part of society which is nearest the patient, his own family. Without trying to reduce his patient's illness to his complexes, still less to the complexes of those around him, he is nevertheless forced to question them, or rather to help them to question themselves regarding their own fundamental attitudes. We will only mention here in this context the role played today by group psychotherapy for the mothers of schizophrenics. The Freudian invitation to examine oneself in the presence of another is at the heart of modern psychiatry, not as an obsession, but as an obvious need, a habit to be formed, a fundamental attitude of benevolent neutrality to be acquired, and a becoming aware of everything which might prevent the transference from being established in the first place and the relationship from being brought to normal after that, and this even in the case of the psychotic patient.

But the Freudian invitation to sincerity goes further—the unconscious, and therefore our unconscious, is in the long run Freud's greatest discovery. Ultimately Freud invites us to consider the truthfulness of what we say, both to ourselves and to others. A neurosis is a lie as well as a repression. This is one of Freud's empirical discoveries and a discovery of a quite new kind: the mentally ill person is no longer to be regarded as a passive sufferer; he is now an active participant in a dialogue between two persons.

But the truthfulness of the discussion and the unmasking of the slips and omissions, which is the essential Freudian requirement, is not only going to illuminate the field of pathology. The question is also put to man and his culture. If psychoanalysis does not make any pronouncement on the subject of human values, it at least questions man about his sincerity with regard to them. It becomes more difficult to confuse virtue and fear, true morality and that which goes no further than that of the scribes and pharisees, which, as Hegel says: is 'envy under the cloak of morality'.

The neurotic implications of art, religion and social life can no longer escape the question Freud puts to them, except through our deliberate fault or through our weakness. Freud could not question neurosis without also questioning culture.

How can the dialogue ever stop?

SYMBOLIC BEHAVIOUR AND THE METAMORPHOSES OF INSTINCT

Professor Charles Baudouin

I. From the association of ideas to psychoanalysis

How is it that ideas or sensory representations get associated so that one will call up another without there being any rational link between them, and in spite of all voluntary effort? The nineteenth-century English school known as Associationism, which included Hamilton and John Stuart Mill, was particularly interested in this question. The laws of association by contiguity, similarity and opposition which were formulated by this school are known today to every student. Two representations evoke each other when their objects have been seen side by side, or when they resemble each other or are opposed to each other. The weakness of the association of ideas theory is the supposition that this play of representations can be explained by the intrinsic character of the representations themselves. It gradually came to be realized that the theory was inadequate and that it was necessary to invoke other causes, external to the representations; in fact, emotional causes.

It was with Ribot, at the end of the nineteenth century, that this appeal to the emotional factor became explicit. It was Ribot who drew attention to two important facts, which he called condensation and transference. Condensation refers to 'emotional associations' or amalgams of representations which have come together and fused for the sole reason that their objects were surrounded by the same affective state and characterized by a 'common affective tone' of joy, sadness, love, hate, etc. Ribot added with great insight that 'this form of association is very frequent in dreams and fantasy'. Transference means that a feeling has been transferred from its original object to some associated object, for example from a beloved person to her clothes or house, or from a saint to a relic.

These two facts were soon to stand out in the foreground of Freud's psychoanalysis. Freud was particularly interested in the study of dreams,[1] and discovered that condensation (*Verdichtung*) was a consistent factor. As to transference (*Übertragung*), this term became of very great importance in Freud's eyes because of his masterly insight into the idea of repression (*Verdrängen*), by means of which the real object of a feeling may become unconscious, while the objects on to which the feeling has been transferred are completely substituted for it in consciousness. It is no longer a question of a mere broadening, but of an actual displacement (*Verschiebung*) of the feeling; traditional psychology knew nothing of this transference mechanism because its most fundamental forms, being fundamental, and unconscious, were never observed.

II. *The evolution of instinct*

Freud, concerned as he was with hysterics, was led, as everybody knows, to study the displacement of sexual impulses and feelings, and to conclude that suppressed sexual behaviour can find substitute satisfaction in neurosis or perversion or, more happily, in moral, intellectual, aesthetic or religious sublimation.

Certainly, the further the derived object is from the original object of the instinct, the more contestable the fact would seem to be. The methodological principle according to which the existence of such transformations is established ought to be formulated all the more clearly. It could be formulated as follows:

[1] From the time of his first major work, the *Traumdeutung*, 1900.

We have already said that condensation between the sensory representations of two objects (we shall in future say between two objects, for the sake of simplicity) arises from a similarity in their affective tone. But we see condensations arising from two objects characterized by affective states which seem to have no bearing on each other, as in those dreams, familiar to all investigators, which seem to associate in a most distressing manner such things as sexuality and aesthetic pleasure or an exhibition of nakedness with the affirmation of personal dignity. In order to understand condensations such as these one is forced to postulate some vital relationship, of which the subject is unconscious, between the two emotional states concerned. In cases such as these, where a crude instinctive tendency is associated with a tendency of a higher kind the only way to understand the relationship between the two affective states is in terms of development. The hypothesis of this relationship is verified:

1. when the life history of the subject shows that the development of the second tendency follows a partial or total suppression of the first;

2. better still, when the same condensation and the same historical development occur in many subjects.

By following these principles, which are only too often taken for granted by psychoanalysts and which gain from being made explicit, a consistent verification may be obtained of many of the most daring views advanced by Freud in connection with the transformation of the sexual instinct in the human psyche.

At about the same time animal psychologists, such as Auguste Forel, came to reject the old belief in the fixity of instincts. They had observed suppression and transformation of instinct. Thanks to psychoanalysis these two facts may also be affirmed of man, and in man the transformations are particularly numerous and flexible. Further, a link has been established between these two facts: suppression is only apparent and is the supreme condition of transformation. An instinct which is transformed is above all an instinct which has been thwarted.

It is difficult to deny that today the sexual instinct is one of the most powerful, and also one of those on which social and civilized life places the most constraint, and this is enough fully to justify Freud's position in giving such an unwavering attention to the transformation of the energy of this instinct, energy which he calls *libido*. Briefly, he rediscovered through his clinical experience the Platonic theory of the metamorphoses of Eros.

However that may be, the only fundamental datum from which we can start is condensation which, on the level of emotion and instinct or, to use one word, of tendencies, uncovers for us deep relationships between elements which on the surface seem quite distinct. Psychoanalysis succeeded in discovering relationships between tendencies similar to those which the evolutionists had noticed between biological species. This comparison is instructive.

It will be remembered that the theory of evolution rests on the contributions made by three sciences; comparative anatomy, paleontology and embryology. Comparative anatomy perceived that there were striking similarities between the organs of different species; paleontology fixed the order of appearance, and so established the relationship between the species; embryology shows that the embryo in higher animals reproduces in epitome the same order of development that is discovered by paleontology. Now psychoanalysis is above all a comparative anatomy of tendencies; it discovers the relationship between facts which have some resemblance to those of embryology, and it is only able to do this when it can establish in a subject the existence of a number of tendencies and the history of their transformation; finally it attempts, notably with Jung and his followers, dizzy excavations into the paleontological levels of primitive thought and the 'collective unconscious' and exhumes mythical monsters which, curiously enough, seem to live again in the childhood stages of the individual psyche. There is good ground for hope, even for ambitious ideas, but it is true that all these investigations are still in their first stages and are still far from being without gaps: when we are trying to trace the family tree of tendencies, there is still room for many hypotheses and great caution is called for. If this were remembered more often the psychoanalytical experts would not provide us with the spectacle described by the great Claparède, who was one of the first French-speaking psychologists to grasp the importance of the new science: 'They confuse hypothesis with fact and disregard the method of systematic doubt, and they all too easily imagine that a theory is a profession of faith. They may also be seen in the grip of internal quarrels, divided up into little enemy factions, hermetically closed to the profane, which they regard with a half-hidden smile of contented superiority, as if they were the hierophants of some esoteric doctrine. But these are human weaknesses.'[1]

These lines were written in 1921. It must be admitted that they have not lost much either of their relevance or of their freshness.

But is there nothing here but 'human weakness'? It would seem that in this particular case there are particular susceptibilities and intolerances, perhaps themselves analysable. We have already, in *De l'Instinct à l'Esprit*, pointed out the direction we think the search should take. The unconscious corresponds to what was previously called the occult; if one is not very careful it is enough to touch this mysterious and forbidden thing for the whole gamut of esoteric

[1] These lines are taken from the preface with which Claparède presented Yves Le Lay's French translation of Freud's *Five Lectures on Psycho-Analysis* (Sonor, Geneva, 1921), a publication which marks a date, and which seems to have been decisive in the matter of the penetration of Freudian ideas into France. This passage shows that our teacher, unafraid of compromising himself, played a powerful stroke in favour of these new ideas, then seen in such lack of perspective, without losing any of his own clarity, independence of thought, and fine critical spirit. It is there complete: the boldness and caution of the true scholar. We have tried to remain faithful to this double lesson.

and fanatical behaviour to be set off like a reflex action.[1]

III. Symbols

This is where the study of condensation has brought us, and it can be seen it is quite a long way. If we take up the second of the two basic facts with which we started our account, displacement, we shall see that this also has ramifications which are no less important, and no less fruitful in suggestion.

For symbolism is grounded on displacement. We have already said that in dreams the emotional charge tends to become displaced from its own object on to an associated one; hostile feeling directed to the father is discharged, in this way, against a substitute for the father, such as a leader or a king. This figure may be called a symbol of the father. Interpretation proceeds by way of a detailed examination of all the subject's constant association systems. For the symbolism of dreams and fantasy results from an emotional displacement similar to those displacements which we have already seen to take place in real life. A comparison of these two facts, symbolism and displacement, at first sight so different, seemed to us to be very illuminating, and we set ourselves to make a detailed study of their relationship. Here, in brief, is the result of this investigation:

The substitutions which give rise to the use of particular symbols do not happen by chance. Suppose that an object A (the father) is replaced in a dream by an object B (a fierce animal). There is certainly some reason for the choice of this second object. What is it? This problem did not engage Freud's attention as much as might have been expected because his attention was directed elsewhere, to the process of disguising in dreams: the important thing for a dream is to

[1] The two preceding sections summarize the ideas developed in our *Introduction à l'Analyse des Rêves*, 1945 (3rd edition, L'Arche, Paris); the two following sections summarize ideas developed in *L'Ame et l'Action* (Mont-Blanc, Geneva, 1945) and in *De l'Instinct à l'Esprit* (Desclée de Brouwer, Bruges-Paris, 1950).

disguise the repressed object A and anything serves for this purpose—as one stops up a hole with whatever is at hand. This explanation of symbolism by the mechanism of disguising cannot be entirely rejected, but it has been losing ground.[1] The problem, then, remains: the substitute object B is not just anything; for example, we often notice the substitution of a fierce animal for the father. If in a large number of cases notice is taken of the objects which serve as a symbol for the father, the frequent repetition of a fairly narrow range of objects is quite striking.

If these objects are arranged in a list we get what we suggest calling a symbolic system—in this particular case the symbolic system of the father. This system includes, among others, the terms: father, brother, uncle, godfather, master, leader, sovereign, state, God, authority, and in another direction the whole array of fierce animals, such as the bear, the lion, the eagle, the horse (all of which occur in coats of arms!). These elements are universally met with in the father system. Beyond this each subject modifies the system for himself by adding personal elements, taken from his own experience but closely associated with those we have mentioned. The same applies to all the symbolic systems.

However, it does not seem to us quite accurate to regard the various terms of the system as substitutes for one of them, the term father. As things are at present it would seem more cautious simply to regard them as being in some way or another emotionally equivalent and capable of being substituted one for another. This reduces the danger of prejudging the issue and here, in our opinion, it is necessary to consider the position of the early psychoanalytic theories with regard to this point. It is true that in some cases it is easily seen which of the two given terms is the more primitive, and which

[1] We first cast doubt on this explanation in our *Études de Psychanalyse*, 1922. Since then Piaget has written a great deal to the same effect. Cf. our discussion of this subject in *L'Ame enfantine et la Psychanalyse*, 2nd edition, volume II, p. 174 (Delachaux & Niestlé, Neuchâtel–Paris, 1951).

indicates a more advanced stage of development. For instance the term father is doubtless more primitive than abstract words like state or authority, although some sociological findings even call this in question. But in other cases it is more difficult to decide.[1]

Let us take, for example, the curious symbolic system which we can call the virility system, and which includes a number of quite different objects: virility in the sexual sense, and virility in a general sense (courage, boldness, power, etc.), aggressiveness, the male sexual organ, a whole series of objects associated with this one on account of their shape (long or pointed objects, etc.) but which are usually associated as well with the idea of aggression (snake, stick, sword, revolver, cannon, weapons in general); then, in other directions: the head, the right hand, self-assertion, personality, family name, etc. To ask which in this case is the basic term may well lead to confusion. This question has in fact given rise to an important divergence of views. For Freud the basic term in this system is the phallus, while Adler looks for it in the more abstract direction of self-assertion or power. That is to say, in the first school of thought all the various terms would be phallic symbols, and in the second they would be symbols of power. The same ambiguity marks the system which is the opposite of the one we have been discussing, the one which we call the mutilation system. This includes ideas and imagery as diverse as castration, decapitation, a broken column, the breaking or snatching away of weapons, impotence, inferiority. For Freud these different things all represent castration, for Adler they represent inferiority; the castration complex of the one corresponds to the inferiority complex of the other; it is the same system, but they start from opposite ends.

[1] It would be relevant to apply here Lévy-Brühl's teaching on primitive mystical complexes, which has been used as a basis for our symbolic systems and the reflections we have been able to make on this subject. Cf. *L'Ame et l'Action*, ch. III.

Another example may be found in the recent history of psychoanalysis; the abandonment complex, introduced by Charles Odier and Germaine Guex, links up from a more social point of view with what has long been known among traditional psychoanalysts, under a more biological aspect, as the weaning complex. Again it is the same system, with a new approach, which as a matter of fact has proved a fruitful one. The relationship between weaning and abandonment is much the same as that between the Freudian castration and the Adlerian inferiority. The fact, moreover, that the supporters of the abandonment theory have not had to put up with the anathemas which had earlier been hurled at the Adlerians would seem to show that 'orthodox' susceptibility has lessened since the heroic period described by Claparède in the passage we have just considered.

The question of discovering which is the basic term of a system is in any case not an easy one, and it is usually framed incorrectly, not being made sufficiently explicit. What should be understood by the expression, basic term? Does it mean the original term, the oldest, from which the development started, or does it mean the term which is the most important at present? Moreover, the importance depends on one's point of view. One gets the impression that Freud implicitly looks for the oldest and that his frame of reference is the life of the individual, whereas Adler is trying to find which is the most important from the social point of view. It looks as if the choice of a basic term will always involve a certain degree of arbitrariness. To the same extent, but only to that extent, can interpretations of a dream, for example, based on the conscientious study of the subject's systems of association be said to be arbitrary. But these divergencies, which result from badly framed or premature questions, should not be allowed to discredit the well established conclusions out of which the divergency arose. These conclusions are expressed in terms of the symbolic systems. Divergence only takes place when it is said that one term symbolizes another in the sense of disguising it, as if only the term symbolized were true; but this conception, itself resulting from the fact that Freud was in the first place interested in this disguising, is defective. It is more accurate to say that the different terms in a symbolic system can all symbolize each other. It is therefore preferable to designate each system, so far as may be done, by a general name, which does not prejudge the question of the basic term: and so we prefer the word mutilation to the too narrowly sexual word castration, and the too abstract word inferiority. It is above all desirable not to confuse symbolism with disguising, which is only a particular case of it or an incidental result of it. Looked at in this way, analytic psychology, freed from improperly framed or premature questions and from sterile discussion, can advance on firm ground.

IV. Transference and symbols

Having settled this point, let us return to our problem: what is the relationship between the symbolism used in dreams and the transference observed in real life? We can in the first place formulate this

1st law of displacement:

A transference of emotion takes place between objects which for the subject belong to the same symbolic system.

The transference, therefore, leads to behaviour that is truly symbolic: such and such a hostile act against a leader or against the state will be an indication of hostility towards the father, and will discharge this hostility. Let us remark in passing that it is when we look at things from the point of view of behaviour, an approach that since Janet has proved a very fruitful one for psychology, that we suddenly see before our eyes this illuminating relationship between transference and symbols; for dream symbols are themselves, in our opinion, rudimentary actions.

But then, in view of this striking similarity, it will be asked, rather, what distinguishes these two cases from each other. This is the answer:

If a comparison is made between a subject's dreams and fantasies on the one hand, and the emotional transferences which have taken place in his everyday life on the other, it will be seen that both one and the other take place within the same symbolic systems. But, in real life, transference only involves a few of the terms in the system, and the emotions are attached to these terms in a fairly stable manner. Only a few terms are retained in real life, widely separated from each other, and their relationship would not have been noticed if nothing but actual behaviour was in question. But dreams run through all the intermediate terms, negotiating all the transitions and allowing us to reconstitute the whole chain. Herein lies their value; through the virtual behaviour that they initiate they throw a light on actual behaviour.

The question arises whether there are no intermediate situations to be found. Indeed there are, in play. The child who plays is day-dreaming, but his dream is less free than when he is asleep, and more closely connected with actual objects. But even so, what freedom is possible! What ease in passing from one object to another! It is easy to trace several typical series of displacements: a child starts by liking to play with mud, or even with excrement, and progressively displaces his interest on to earth, sand, pebbles, collections of stones, and finally collections of medals.

On the basis of stability, or, if preferred, of increasing viscosity or decreasing fluidity, it is valid to go on from there to place in series:

1. dream displacements, multiple and instantaneous, with their functions of disguise and discharge;
2. displacements in play, found in games and also in art, with the function of exercise as well as that of discharge;
3. transferences made in real life.

It is legitimate to summarize the foregoing remarks and formulate the

2nd law of displacement:

The ease of displacement, otherwise called the mobility of affective energy, decreases as we pass from dreams to play and from play to real life.

From which it may reasonably be supposed that one of the functions of dreams, play and art is to maintain the mobility of energy and avoid emotional crystallization, so that fresh possibilities may be continually tried out.

V. Psychoanalysis and art

These reflections lead up to our final considerations on the remarkable perspective taken on by art and poetry when they are illuminated by psychoanalysis.

In the first place works of art, like dreams, are certainly a privileged object of analysis; they, like dreams, are a form of symbolic behaviour. Freud opened the way to this psychoanalysis of art with a few brief studies; Rank threw himself into it with intensity; for some time now these pioneers have been followed by many others.

But one must take care not to think, as some people have done, that this analysis will be reductive, that is to say that it will show that art is 'nothing but...' and that the enchantment of art will be destroyed. Analysis applied to the creative artist would no doubt modify his art; afterwards he would, perhaps, work in another style; but a true vocation would not be destroyed.

In any case, Freud and his pupils have always had a very strong sense of art as expression and as knowledge; they have continually drawn attention to the penetrating insight into human nature shown by the Greek tragedians, Shakespeare and the great novelists, an insight which was psychoanalytic before the word was thought of, from which it would appear that it is to this kind of writer that the new psychology should look for its precursors and teachers, rather than to the academic psychologists.[1]

Let us add that just as analysing the individual artist does not destroy his talent, but transforms it, in the same way applying analysis to art itself does not 'reduce it' to anything; but it does run the risk of giving it a direction by laying down the basis of an aesthetics. However, ideas are in the air. It is striking to note that the symbolist movement in poetry preceded the birth of psychoanalysis by only a few years. We are being led by different paths to an aesthetics in which art takes full cognisance of its symbolic function, although understanding quite well that symbols are not metaphors, in which one term more or less arbitrarily signifies a second, but that they are symphonies in which a number of terms are organically related to each other; the reflections of a Mallarmé on the multiple meaning of poetry fit in remarkably well with our psychology of condensation and the multiple meaning of dreams. It may be that classical symbolism has degenerated into period mannerisms and decadent affectations quite foreign to its essential inspiration and to its discovery of the symbol; it may be that the surrealism which followed it wandered off into a dead end and that its explicit reference to psychoanalysis was for the most part based on a misunderstanding. But look, for example, at Carl Spitteler, a great poet of the German language, who sprang up untouched by the formula of any school; a contemporary of Nietzsche and Freud, related to them rather than influenced by them, solitary like a monolith, he must have exercised a justifiable influence over many psychoanalysts. His novel *Imago* shares with Sophocles' *Oedipus* the honour of having become a technical term in the new science, and it is also the title of an

---

[1] We have tried to keep this double point of view in our psychoanalytic studies on art, particularly in the *Triomphe du Héros* (Plon, Paris, 1951), where we think we have been able to disengage the human meaning of the myth underlying the great epic poems.

important psychoanalytic review. He succeeded in reuniting himself with the living myth, rising from the unconscious, and integrating it with consciousness in luminous Apollonian symbols, in which can be seen the call to a new classicism, a symbolic classicism. We have already had occasion to say that one of the best introductions to depth psychology would be to read his amazing *Prometheus and Epimetheus*[1] and then Jung's important commentary on it in *Psychological Types*.

We mean to make it clear by these last remarks that psychoanalysis does not turn its gaze towards art in order to depreciate it. Psychoanalysis not only regards art as one of its privileged objects of study, but also sees, in this highly symbolic behaviour, intuitions worthy of being taken seriously by the scholar engaged in exploring the human mind, who cannot help but gain in allowing himself to be guided by them, provided he will translate them and arrange them in his own framework of facts and laws. In this way psychoanalysis is re-discovering, by other ways and in another light, the old Platonic truth that knowledge is to be found in myths, those living and spontaneous symbols of vital human situations.

[1] London, 1931.

THE PSYCHOANALYST

Dr Charles-Henri Nodet

The Freudian psychoanalyst is not a doctor like other doctors. From one point of view this is quite obvious, as everybody knows that there are psychoanalysts, some of them famous, who are not medically qualified, and that this has Freud's explicit approval. Some people would like to conclude from this that the practice of psychotherapy cannot be regarded as coming within the domain of medicine.

It is true that psychotherapeutic practice, viewed strictly as a technique, depends primarily on psychological knowledge and judgement, which are within the competence of an adequately trained layman without medical qualifications.

It is also true that the atmosphere of psychotherapy is rather like that of education, since the subject—we no longer think of him literally as a patient—plays an active role, indispensable to the success of the treatment. The subject takes his recovery upon himself, which is quite different from the passivity with which, in ordinary medicine, anyone who is ill is expected to accept the authority and prescriptions of the person who is treating him.

However, this also is true: even if the therapy is carried out for a time within a purely psychological framework (and in some cases this is the longest and most important part of the treatment) it remains no less deeply rooted in the unity of diagnostic and clinical psychiatry, and no less closely connected with all the other kinds of therapy.

All the same the psychoanalyst, in so far as he is a psycho-analyst, is not a doctor like other doctors. The main proof of this lies in his training, which requires him to undergo a personal analysis. This analysis, although called a teaching analysis, is in fact therapeutic. It is another departure from the traditional field for it to be considered necessary for a doctor to submit himself in the first place to the treatment which later on he will in his turn administer. But we have discovered a certain law of human relationship: that when we enter into contact with other people we cannot give them what we do not ourselves possess, and this applies also to mental balance; in order to be able to do anything worth while with another person a certain facility of being at his service is required, and this is not necessarily given by com-mon sense, good will and theoretical knowledge, even psychi-atric knowledge.

The psychoanalyst is therefore bound up with his tech-nique to a much greater extent than if it were a straight-forward method of investigation or a kindly handing out of helpful advice. The analyst, above all, gives what he is, because he is involved in a dialogue, with his patient, and just as much as his patient. Two complete personalities face each other, each composed of conscious and unconscious: the analyst must not lose himself, and the person being analysed should in the end find himself.

It is therefore impossible to speak of the analyst without speaking of psychoanalysis and considering some of its general principles in so far as they put the therapeutic practice, and therefore the therapy itself, into perspective.

We can summarize the essentials of the treatment in the following three points:

1. The vital nexus of the therapeutic process is expressed in the following proposition: there is a liberating value in the subject's becoming aware of the hidden psychic life which, all unknown to him, has been motivating him and controlling his symptoms.

The subject has to become aware not only of the feelings and memories which have been forgotten or evaded, but also of the protective mechanisms, repression, devaluation and isolation, which have kept them out of consciousness.

It is not usual now to set out on a systematic search for traumatic childhood memories. Nowadays the breaking of the childhood amnesia is thought to result from the progress of the treatment, rather than as causing this progress, although the two processes may well interact.

2. The most important thing is the analysis of the subject's behaviour during the course of the session, and the dynamic modifications which this analysis sets going. For the subject reacts to the analytic situation in terms of the permanent dispositions of his make-up. The more closely certain patterns of behaviour correspond to earlier experiences which were cut short, the more will he repeat them, and the more successfully the analyst's professional neutrality prevents fuel being provided by the present situation, the purer will this repetition be. The analysis of these transference reactions is the corner stone of the whole treatment, and this is one of Freud's most original contributions.

By becoming aware of the regressive, that is childish, elements in his make-up the subject, as it were, restarts his arrested emotional development. Once the protective mechanisms are thoroughly shaken, and the subject is able to see and express in the course of the dialogue the level of immaturity at which he is really living, recovery takes place suddenly, like a life shooting up with renewed impetus toward its natural flowering. The analytic treatment leads the subject to discover by experience that his strength and riches lie, in the first place, in his becoming aware in the presence of another person of that weakness and poverty which for so long he has been employing all his resources to hide, and which, after all, consist of nothing but childhood experiences which were broken off unfinished and which only need light

and a little talking to enable them to reach their own completion in a higher stage of maturity.

3. The analyst, then, plays a double role. In the first place
he is that other person in front of whom the subject has to
place himself, and bring into play all the fears and self-
complacency which enter into his make-up. But, besides
playing the role of a questioner, who in any case is often
silent, the analyst has to interpret the situation, and enable
the subject to discover the exact significance of his own part
in the dialogue. This discovery of himself by himself is the
aim of all the analyst's interventions, and the fruit of his un-
tiring work of interpretation.

This work on the part of the analyst raises all kinds of
problems. The most obvious find their answers in that corpus
of psychological knowledge which the analyst has to master
and to which he will always be adding. From this point of
view the analyst needs to know his trade, as any practitioner
needs to know the theory underlying his particular practice.
There is no need to linger on this point.

But in contrast to this the double role we have just been
talking about lends a particular character to the work of the
analyst and the qualities which he must bring to it. There is
question of human value, of all the human values involved
in the analytic situation and in the work of interpretation.

The analytic situation brings the analyst into play as well
as the person he is analysing, the unconscious of the one as
well as that of the other. The transference reactions of the
analysand have to be answered by the reactions of the counter-transference on the part of the analyst. It is impossible for
there to be no such counter-transference reactions, because
the analyst is himself engaged in this human relationship of
the analytic dialogue. But these reactions should be clearly
recognized and kept within limits, otherwise there will be a
serious risk of their surreptitiously distorting the free play of
the intuition, attention and memories with which the analyst
carries out his interpretation. We shall come back to this later.

But in any case the work of interpretation would be quite impossible without some frame of reference. Every time that the analyst draws the subject's attention to some aspect or other of what he has said or done, he does so in the light of certain co-ordinates of that human nature whose solidity should form an integral part of our common heritage.[1] To look for a hidden meaning implies that the apparent meaning is inadequate, and it can only be judged inadequate if a definite position has been taken up, affective, rational or moral.

This is a very delicate point which we cannot let pass without going into a little, because this is where a serious criticism of the analyst is liable to be made: that he may impress his own personal system of values upon his patient. The analyst would then become a teacher and guide, with regard to feelings and even to thought, which would be a crushing and a very controversial responsibility.

If it is to be of any use at all, any interpretive work must suppose a certain tacit agreement between doctor and patient.

For example, the patient is not very clear what he is letting himself in for when he accepts as binding the fundamental rule of sincerity in all he says. But it is also necessary to point out that it is not only that the patient has agreed to say everything; he will also be forced, by the development of the treatment and the attitude of the analyst in interpreting, to recognize that every attempt, conscious or not, to side-track this sincerity, is a personal problem with a meaning, inviting him to press on towards the ultimate psychological truth about himself. There is in this a certain sense of truth which will impregnate many of the interpretations. The analyst will make use of this sense of truth without ever imposing it dictatorially on his patient. It may be mentioned in this context that psychoanalysis always takes the optimistic line of never proclaiming values, knowing that they are there all

[1] Dr Nodet, 'Quelques réflexions sur les valeurs engagées dans la cure analytique,' *Revue française de Psychanalyse*, 1957.

the time and are only waiting to be freed from their fetters to develop of themselves. It must be admitted, however, that it is essential for these values to be present at least in a rudimentary state, from the very beginning of the analysis, otherwise no interpretive work will be possible. Real depravity and certain character neuroses are not amenable to analysis, since the fundamental psychological structure is either non-existent or unusable.

But even more often than he appeals to the sense of truth, the psychoanalyst speaks to what may be called a certain sense of unity. For it is necessary to be able to count on the subject's wanting to have some sort of logic in his thoughts and feelings, desiring it and regarding it as a better state. The analyst assumes the right to point out an instance of false reasoning, a flagrant contradiction or an ambiguous expression, not to blame the subject for it but so that he may be shaken by his own faulty thinking. This sense of truth and sense of unity may be regarded as mental structures which will certainly be developed by the analysis, but which must be there in embryo from the beginning as the necessary instruments without which no analysis can be undertaken or satisfactorily conducted.

Besides, psychoanalysis thinks of a neurosis primarily as an emotional retardation, and this involves a certain conception of adult emotional life. Analytic experience cannot reject the idea of progress and development without abjuring itself, any more than educational experience can. The term of this development is not something theoretical, but something discovered experimentally; it is the term which is seen to be sufficient to prevent neurotic trouble arising, and that towards which the patient under treatment is working as his symptoms disappear.

This development corresponds to a genitalization of the sexual impulses, enabling a person to achieve a full heterosexual maturity and at the same time an untroubled and constructive socialization of his emotions of love and aggression. The subject then reaches an autonomy which allows him a degree of emotional independence, since he no longer has to rely on other people's love and approval in order to maintain his own integrity without anxiety. This contribution from other people, however valuable it may be, is no longer demanded or expected as a vital necessity; it is this demanding and expectation which indicate the persistence of a childhood dependence full of aggressiveness. In other words, whatever disappointment or privation life may bring, it will no longer be experienced as an intolerable frustration, releasing either anxiety or some character trait to serve as a protection against this anxiety.

These rather lengthy remarks seem necessary in order to put the analyst in perspective both with regard to his patient and with regard to the general problems raised by the therapeutic dialogue.

The important innovation, which we spoke about earlier on, is that the psychoanalyst's training requires a certain readjustment of his own personality, to enable him to understand and to control this relationship between two people which is the mark of all psychotherapy but of psychoanalysis in particular.[1] This is the purpose of what is called a teaching analysis.

1. In the first place the teaching analysis provides practical experience of the relationship between two people which he will form later on in his analytic contact with his patient. The presence of a third person would be a fatal impediment to the purity of such a situation. In order to learn how to understand it, one must of necessity pass through it oneself. This analysis takes place under the same conditions as any other analysis: four or five sessions a week, of forty-five to fifty minutes each, usually for at least two years. In addition to this, the newly qualified analyst gets practice at the be-

[1] Michael Balint, 'La formation de l'omnipraticien en psychothérapie', in *Cahiers Laënnec*, Hygiène Mentale, I – 1957, p. 29.

ginning by carrying out controlled analyses, generally two in
number, in order to benefit from the experience of an older
man: he conducts them alone with his patient but each week
he reports to his tutor what he has heard and what he has
understood, how and when he has intervened.

2. Theoretical knowledge alone does not enable vital contact to be made with a patient, and this applies in the analytic field perhaps more than anywhere else. It is possible to
get a fairly accurate idea of a fracture of the neck of the femur
from a textbook and to recognize one when one sees it, even
if one has never seen it previously, but one cannot learn from
a textbook how to listen to the heart, and even listening to
recordings does not dispense one from a long apprenticeship.
A castration complex only develops in concrete social situations, and one cannot recognize the living reality until one
has experienced it among one's own problems. Analytic
knowledge is above all experimental knowledge, a lived experience before which all theoretical knowledge should recognize its limits.

3. The teaching analysis is more than an apprenticeship,
it is also a therapeutic analysis. We are not talking about the
would-be therapist who has obvious neurotic symptoms of
which he wishes to be rid. We are speaking of candidates who
would be regarded as reasonably well balanced in the light
of sound psychiatric judgement. Analytic medicine requires
more than this. Apart from the classic clinical neuroses there
is the whole immense array of character neuroses and neurotic character traits, character traits which on the face of it
seem quite ordinary. There is no question of seeing mental
illness everywhere, but experience shows how these personality traits are formed. Without denying the part played by
heredity and bodily constitution, it may be admitted that
many elements of the personality have been acquired during
childhood as formations which have been developed, with
more or less success, to deal with the problems which arise
at the various stages. One of the surest signs that a particular

personality trait has its origins in some complex, whether sexual or aggressive, is fixity and rigidity.

The teaching analysis does not presume or wish to make any fundamental alteration in the candidate's personality; it is intended to draw his attention to the unsolved problems indicated by some particular character trait, to help him find out what sort of anxiety this character trait is protecting him from when it leads him, often unconsciously, to adopt such and such an attitude towards people or things.

Bringing things to light in this way softens up the character trait in question and often results in its complete disappearance. But this bringing things to light is necessary, above all, to make them available to the patient, and to the particular problems he may bring. If, for example, the doctor has not satisfactorily resolved his own childish aggressiveness towards his father he is liable to recognize this problem only imperfectly in his patient, even if he has personally used his own smouldering resentment as a spur towards a perfectly good professional or social achievement. With the best of intentions he will forget all the allusions his patient may make to a problem he himself is trying to forget.

His analysis as a whole will have taught him how to commit himself without reserve and without anxiety in the presence of this other person who is his analyst. He will have undergone the experience of recognizing those unpalatable truths which indicate one's limitations, and he will have discovered that failure should not lead either to self-depreciation or to an attitude in which one tries to deny the existence of the failure. He will have found out by experience that the strength of the grown-up person lies in being able to consider one's own imperfections without anxiety or self-complacency and in being able to recognize and make allowance for the childish residues of one's own development, without unbearable pain or scornful cynicism.

Bringing things to light by analysis will have been of therapeutic value in as much as those regressive elements which have been honestly admitted will have been helped towards a higher degree of maturity. Certain temperaments will never progress sufficiently to be good psychotherapists, but it is useful to point out that, even for the others, there is a limit to the psychological balance which can be reached. This balance is a living thing which up to a point re-forms itself before each of life's problems. Is it necessary to say that to imagine oneself perfectly and finally balanced would be to return to a deplorably childish absolute? We may add that an analyst is well advised to make a cross-section of personal analysis every five or ten years.

Having made clear in this way the term to which the analyst should be led by his own analysis, and the term to which he should, by the same method, lead his patient, we are in a better position to grasp certain fundamental attitudes which the analyst should have, and to understand the reasons for them.

It is traditional, since Freud, to speak of the floating attention of the analyst, and of his benevolent neutrality, which means in practice that the analyst will limit his contact with his patient to the sessions themselves, and will avoid any social relationship outside these sessions. He will listen and will not give advice or express an opinion; he will limit himself to interpreting his patient's behaviour and to re-establishing the psychological links between the present and the past. This neutrality, which has led to the attitude of the analyst being compared to a mirror, which reflects back to the person being analysed whatever he projects on to it, is qualified by the word benevolent because it gives the patient to understand that everything in the analyst is at his service. This is expressed by an unwavering attention, and even by means of a silence which the patient may regard in the first place as a rejection, but the irreplaceable value of which he will gradually come to appreciate, as he begins to recognize in it first the permission, then the possibility, and finally the freedom to be completely himself. This attention is called floating, in as much as the analyst is required to accept everything, and not, in the first place, to make any selection —he never takes notes—because he knows that it is often behind the words and between the lines that the patient really expresses himself.

This preliminary sketch of the analyst, interpreting what the patient, unknown to himself, projects on to this neutrality, accepting and reflecting like a mirror, needs to be filled in and made more precise.

1. In the first place this neutrality is a limiting concept and the success of the treatment often requires that it should not be carried to its theoretical point of absolute rigidity. In any case this is impossible. 'On this mirror which the analyst has accepted as his role there is a faint tracing of his own personality: it is this outline, composed as it is of infinitesimal perceptions, and not an inhuman emptiness, which forms the background against which the projected images of the transference properly so-called will display themselves.'[1] It cannot be denied that the analyst has a temperament, an intellectual background, an apartment, charges a fee, etc. and it would be foolish to ignore the part played by these things in the analytic situation, however much one may wish to minimize them.

More important is the 'presence'[2] which is already a stable reality in so far as the analyst keeps his interpretations at a certain level. But there comes a stage of the analysis when the patient has to recognize the existential reality of this other man with whom he has been carrying on a dialogue for so many months. Sometimes the course of the analysis may make it necessary to draw attention to this presence and to reduce the mystery of the situation to some degree, if the

[1] Dr Michel Gressot, 'Y a-t-il une éthique du Psychanalyste?' Communication to the Société Suisse de Psychiatrie, Schaffouse, 15 June 1957.

[2] Dr S. Nacht, 'Transfert et contretransfert', XVIth Congrès international de Zurich, August 1949, in *Revue française de Psychanalyse*, III, 1949.

patient is using this conventional neutrality to cut himself comfortably off from all emotional contact. The analyst may make use of some chance incident, or he may even intervene directly. Such a careful modification of the neutrality, carried out very tactfully, is sometimes essential in the case of patients with very primitive fixations, such as abandonent neuroses,[1] as the extreme fragility of the ego in those cases would find the frustration imposed by the usual treatment quite intolerable.

2. In the second place the floating attention which the analyst is expected to maintain makes possible a spontaneity of intervention which would be hindered by too strenuous an attempt to consider, compare or remember. The analyst's unconscious plays an essential role, upon which he must be able to rely. This unconscious, permanently on the alert, is composed of various things.

Personal qualities are necessary, although training plays a great part. Accumulated theoretical knowledge and all past experience together form a foundation which is always being enriched. If the analyst listens attentively without attempting a rigid or arbitrary classification of what he hears he will be able to absorb whatever is said, together with its fringe of possible meanings, and have everything readily available for whenever it may be needed. The accumulated results of his work as a whole enables him to follow quite flexibly the sidetracks by which a patient betrays the structure of his neurosis, and the regressive and progressive modifications which punctuate the course of the treatment.

This activity on the part of the analyst takes place at the borderline between his conscious and his preconscious, which is the level at which every technique strengthens itself with habits. It should be as spontaneous and relaxed as possible, both in maintaining a faultless reception and in the initiative of intervening. But this spontaneity, which the analyst needs in order to maintain his contact as a questioner and at the

[1] G. Guex, *La névrose d'abandon*, Paris, P.U.F., 1950.

same time his distance as an observer, is liable to become the easy prey of the underground stirrings of a troubled unconscious. We have already twice alluded to this dangerous and subtle distortion of the analyst's reactions which can take place as the result of an inadequately clarified attitude towards his patient. We are now coming to the principle problem in psychotherapy, the counter-transference.

3. We have seen that the analyst is committed to a human relationship with his patient. We have made it clear that behind the benevolent neutrality of his analyst, the analysand should be able to discern the rich depths of another person, another self, but other than himself.

In his turn the analyst is subject to the same laws and the same risk of subjectivity. He cannot remain ignorant of the fact that behind his patient there is a man like himself, and he ought always to remain clear about what this man means to him, by reason of his personal qualities as well as in his role of questioner or his position as a patient.

The analyst does not have to hide from himself the interest which draws him towards his patient. Complete indifference would be self-deception. It is obviously impossible to cure one's fellow creature without a real attachment both to the art of healing and to the existence of the man himself. To speak of attachment implies the possibilities of satisfaction and disappointment. Failure and success cannot be taken with exactly the same smile. But there are two comments which it is essential to make:

On the one hand this attachment, which, as we have just seen, should be purged of any trace of unsolved complexes, can quite consciously reach such an intensity as to call for some restraint, since it would otherwise interfere with the floating attention the analyst should maintain. One patient is inevitably more likeable than another. But if a continual effort is needed to prevent oneself from being too overwhelmed by spontaneous feelings, friendly, sexual or aggressive, it would be better to shake hands and send the

patient to a colleague. There is a way of being at the service
of another which is stable of itself, without the need for any
effort, even moral effort.[1] A too imperious scientific interest
would be harmful to the patient in much the same way. It is
true that a certain amount of curiosity can help the mind to
keep alert, but nevertheless it is necessary to be able to accept
a real moderation, sometimes quite meritorious. In any case
it has been remarked that it is not always the pioneers who
make the best practitioners.

These conscious reactions are not the most dangerous, and
this brings us to our second observation. Far more dangerous
are those unconscious elements which may disturb the therapist's relationship with his patient despite his integrity and his
attempt to keep everything in the open. Only a teaching analysis, strictly carried out, can reduce this danger, to the extent
that it has been able to free the analyst from the demands
of the complexes that lie hidden behind his character traits,
however attractive these traits may be, or whatever they may
have brought in the way of professional or social success.

We have considered how far it is legitimate to be attached
to the patient one wishes to cure. But it is important that no
unconscious relationship, in which the analyst would be
seeking some hidden advantage, generally aggressive or narcissistic, should be allowed to creep in under cover of this
attachment.

Up to a point the analyst should expect nothing from his
patient, nothing, that is, which might be necessary for his
own mental balance or to calm his own anxiety. A healthy
desire to cure a patient is poles apart from needing the patient,
needing to apply one's knowledge, needing to share in the
recovery. The analyst should have his emotional life well
organized in its essentials quite apart from his patient. He

---

[1] This is not intended as a disparagement of moral effort! There is no
need to emphasize how unworthy it would be to profit from a facile
dependence created by the transference relationship in order to obtain
emotional satisfaction, financial benefit, or anything else.

does not treat others in order to be happy; it is because he is happy, quite apart from his patient, that he is able to treat him and be completely at his service. Some patients have a desperate need to surrender themselves to the psychotherapist: it is a symptom which cannot be analysed unless it recognizes opposite itself another frenzy: 'furor sanandi'. If some of the opposition with which psychoanalysis meets is richer in anxiety than in scientific objectivity, it is nevertheless true that some psychotherapists feel an attraction to the profession which is itself a symptom.

These preliminary remarks on the essential freedom of the analyst with regard to his patient bring us to the central problem, which dominates all neurosis and also affects the conditions under which the treatment develops. This central problem is that of aggressive impulses. An imperfect sublimation gives them, on the phenomenal level, either the thrust of sadism or the withdrawal of masochism. Both these correspond to powerful aggressive forces repressed by equally powerful feelings of guilt. An aggressive attitude gives rise to a compromise situation in which the subject acts aggressively but persuades himself that he is in the right and that he has a good conscience. A passive attitude gives rise to situations from which all overt aggressiveness is excluded. In each case there is the same flight from a guilty impulse.

The aggressiveness is being stifled by feelings of guilt and an essential stage of the treatment is to allow the subject to express it in his conversation. It is necessary for the personality of the analyst to be so structured that he is not afraid of this aggressiveness or of letting it appear. To be more precise, he should not have an unconscious fear of the aggressiveness being directed towards himself. He should never be hurt, however subtle and to the point some displeasing remark may be.[1] One of the most orginal characteristics of psycho-

---

[1] A complimentary remark should be received with the same detachment. To take pleasure in it would divert one from the real problem: what is the true meaning of the remark?

analysis is that, unlike traditional psychotherapy, it refrains from trying to please the patient and from making the treatment seem attractive: this would neutralize the patient's anxiety, and also that of the therapist, but would not permanently solve any serious problem. This unconscious fear of the patient's aggressiveness would badly distort the work of interpretation, by inclining the analyst to forget things, to manipulate the evidence, and even to react emotionally.

If the analyst is afraid of his patient it is because he himself is not at ease with his own aggressiveness. It may happen that he dare not give rein to his spontaneity because it seems to him to be too closely bound up with his own aggressiveness and liable to unlock in himself precisely that aggressiveness which he fears in his patient; or he will perhaps catch himself being either overtly or secretly aggressive in his professional conduct.

It follows that he will be lacking in that respect for the patient which is one of the most basic attitudes expected from an analyst, one which defies all written rules: from this point of view what the therapist says may well count for less than what he is.

If the analyst, instead of keeping his firmness in a state of vital flexibility, lets it get hardened into rigidity by unconscious sadistic traces, he will be liable to direct his conventional neutrality aggressively towards his patient. This quality of flexibility is indispensable both for judging whether an analysis is indicated, and for deciding that an analysis should be drawn to a close. Each case is unique and cannot be treated on a common last, and here, more than elsewhere, the best is the enemy of the good. In analytic terms, perfection, which is a limit towards which the adult is always tending, should not be confused with the childish idea of something absolute, which is a crude and regressive idea.

This respect for the patient requires that the analyst should not try to impose his personal views on him. The analyst should 'enlighten the patient concerning the obstacles in the way of his development, and should free him from them, but he should not give him a blue-print for his future development.'[1] The analyst should consider himself satisfied if he has helped a man to regain his emotional maturity, and need not concern himself with the professional or social use he will make of it. This idea of emotional maturity brings us up against the difficult problem of normality, which is a dangerous concept; but it is equally dangerous to underestimate its importance, both for practice and for theory. The difficulty of keeping this idea free from all trace of arbitrariness must not be minimized, especially as considerations of period, country and intellectual background all enter in. While striving always towards a more precise ideal of the normal, one must take care not to fall into a kind of messianism, an implication, current at one time, that psychoanalysis is a panacea capable of leading men infallibly towards their one true happiness.

This does not prevent the analyst taking account of human values, up to a point, when he considers that maturity which the whole treatment is designed to promote in his patient. There is no point in denying that moral values are involved. Gressot gives a typical example in the article referred to above: 'And so the tendency of the patient to act on his instinctive and characterological propensities, as they emerge, and before they have been integrated into his ego, calls for very careful handling. Only a sufficiently tactful interpretation will enable the patient to take cognizance of the tendency and at the same time prevent it from passing over into an undesirable act.'[2]

This respect for the patient can even be called kindness[3] in the sense that this respect or goodwill patiently waits for him just where we expect him to arrive, in the flowering

[1] Dr Nacht, 'Critères sur la fin du traitement analytique,' *Revue française de Psychanalyse*, 1954, III, p. 334 *et passim*.

[2] Dr Gressot, *loc. cit.*

[3] Dr Nacht, 'Comment terminer le traitement analytique,' *Revue française de Psychanalyse*, 1954, IV, p. 519 *et passim*.

of his own particular personality, and provides him with an unimpeachable witness for his act of self-recognition.

This use of the word kindness, however, should not be allowed to give rise to the slightest misunderstanding. Many therapeutic failures are due to an inextricable entanglement between a transference which has not been properly analysed and a counter-transference which has not been properly recognized and controlled.

This kindness does indeed allow the patient from time to time to experience directly that good object of which, to some degree or other, he was deprived in childhood. But although the analyst should be kind he should never allow himself to fall into the easy habit of giving his patient, necessarily and all the time, that good image which he expects. The analyst must accept the fact that his patient is able to live out his ambivalence and aggressiveness, and needs for therapeutic reasons to take him at certain stages for someone both ill-intentioned and clumsy. In the extreme case it will be with an untroubled heart that the psychotherapist will see his patient deny him the satisfaction of curing him, will see him go off to someone else and straightway get cured, like a woman who will not be happy with the first man in her life, the man who has deflowered her and given her her woman-hood. Gratitude can be too heavy to be borne. True kindness is to think only of the patient's welfare, and not of one's own statistical successes.

This brief account is an attempt to put the psychoanalyst in perspective with regard to his patient: to show him as accepting him and putting himself at his service, which is not possible unless the analyst can listen to him without swallowing up into his own darkness the blind appeals which are made to him.

This patient work most assuredly required intuition, but above all it requires a solid experience, and self-knowledge obtained through a teaching analysis. The analyst distrusts brilliant intuitions and clever improvisations. He has before him the example of some of his patients, whose neurotic tension gives them ultrasensitive antennae, which would seem a most enviable gift were it not for the heavy counter-weight of massive blindness in other directions.

The analyst wants, above all, to be an honest practitioner, trusting in the buried riches of his patient, and the liberating value of a faultless attention.

He may even wonder whether he is not doing his part towards reaffirming the human aspects of medicine, which seem to have been disturbed by the progress of biology and chemistry. The doctor of today is not so sure that the mind and heart call for such exclusively scientific treatment. It is perhaps the anthropological aspect of Freudian psycho-therapy that will enable him to see how, without posing as sage or magician, but also without going back on his own times, he can maintain a personal approach to his patient without prejudice to the strict requirements of science.

THE MAJOR RHYTHMS OF THE PSYCHOANALYTIC TREATMENT

Dr Serge Leclaire

This title was suggested to me by the organizer of the present volume, and although I was given complete freedom to alter it if I chose, I preferred to follow it through the questions it raises for me and to engage the attention of the reader with these same questions, if he will trust himself to come with me. Because, like the patient on the couch, like the interested enquirer who has only too many reasons for feeling shut out, the psychoanalyst himself in his armchair secretly asks himself, 'what is really happening?'

I should really have liked to have left each enquirer to build up a picture for himself of the process that ripens so slowly during those regular sessions on the couch, on the strength of his own private fund of knowledge. But as a result of having kept my ears open (as well as my mouth) at a few crowded cafés I have picked up a certain amount of detailed information from people who ought to know; very often, while busily feeding themselves, they paint a picture of the catharsis and of the relief it brings: at other times it is made clear that after a period during which the old personality is broken down it is necessary to build it up again—something which psychoanalysts would only too often like to forget; being, for my part, sufficiently reconstituted, I left them there. To tell the truth, rather than chatter on in this way, I should have liked to have left a completely blank page, which each one could have filled in as he pleased, from a moral, a logical or a philosophical point of view, according to the bent developed in him by his own particular spirit of enquiry. And if I had been a psychologist, I should have liked to have collected up these various pieces of evidence, because I think they would have been just as useful to the analyst who is trying to understand as the most learned writings.

If we leave the interested enquirer and pass on to the patient, it should be enough similarly for us to gather what he says. Lying on the couch, tired of his questioner's long silence, tempted to protest, he is thinking rapidly. 'I always thought there would have to be a first stage in the treatment during which you would listen without saying anything in order to collect all the facts necessary for an understanding of my case; but I must admit that I am beginning to get impatient to get on to the next stage when you will talk to me at last and tell me what conclusions you have drawn from my long explanations.' Many patients arrive at this opinion at one stage or another of their treatment, and I set it down here with whatever mixture it may contain of truth, neurosis and error.

I am now going to consider the psychoanalyst's point of view, in a double manner; first of all I shall question him in his official capacity—the capacity in which he is accustomed to collaborate in scientific work—that of the practitioner, who will speak, I hope, in a scholarly fashion; but afterwards I shall try to take by surprise that other side of him, sitting yawning in his armchair, fighting his sciatica, trying to follow and understand, doing his best to remain free, and, if he can, a poet.

In order to move about easily in the closed, if not sacred, field of a technique, it is necessary to have a basic, simple and efficient vocabulary. I have therefore quite seriously been thinking that it might be useful to draw up a very short vocabulary of the principal terms commonly used to describe the course of the treatment; besides the accepted meaning (a.m.), considered strictly according to rule, which may not seem very satisfactory to the disrespectful layman, we have added, very briefly, the corresponding meaning from the point of view of criticism and research (res.).

AGGRESSIVENESS: (instinct theory)

a.m.: 'aggressive impulse', which may be sexual or not, innate or acquired.

res.: 'correlative tension of the narcissistic structure in the development of the individual.'[1]

DEFENCE: (dynamic)

a.m.: original function of the ego's control system, by which the ego defends itself against the irruption of the impulses.

res.: moment of a dialectical movement which is always tending towards crystallization.

EGO: (static)

a.m.: the most accessible of the three regions of the personality; organ of control and integration; the chosen object of analysis.

res.: where the subject's imaginative identifications take place.

FRUSTRATION: (dynamic)

a.m.: privation of an instinctive satisfaction.

res.: a complex thing, to be distinguished from privation or lack, and specifically involving purpose.

ID: (static)

a.m.: one of the three agencies of the psychical apparatus, chaos, the source of the impulses.

res.: 'wo Es war soll Ich werden'[2] (literally, where it was, there shall I be.)

[1] Lacan, *Revue Française de Psychanalyse*, 1948, III, p. 375.

[2] Freud, *New Introductory Lectures on Psychoanalysis*, Hogarth Press, 4th impression, 1949, p. 106.

INTERPRETATION: (technique)

a.m.: translation in terms of, or reduction to, a pre-esta-
blished plan.

res.: traditionally, the soothsayer's art.

REGRESSION: (dynamic)

a.m.: return to an earlier stage of libidinal organization.

res.: the period of imaginative fixation dominant at the
moment.

RESISTANCE: (dynamic)

a.m.: concrete manifestation of the defensive attitude within
the framework of the treatment. 'There is no psychoanalysis without analysis of the resistance.'

res.: the 'time to understand' for the therapist, according
to Lacan.

SUPEREGO: (static)

a.m.: regulating agency differentiated from the ego; often
blind, can easily be strict.

res.: law, as conceived by the imagination.

TRANSFERENCE

a.m.: displacement of emotion on to the person of the analyst; reproduction during the analysis of unconscious
emotional attitudes. 'There is no analysis without
transference.'

res.: 'everything irrational which comes up in the analytic
relationship from the beginning' (Bouvet). 'The transference is the time' (Lacan).

Everyone should now be able to follow for himself without
too much trouble the technical account which fidelity to my
title compels me to develop; but it would be more true to say
that I am going to try to reduce it to three points, of which
the first will trace the general rhythm of the treatment, the
second will describe two sequences, and the third will summarize the general idea of how the treatment progresses.

I want to get on to the principal period of the treatment without dwelling on those preliminary questions which are so much discussed in analytic circles, such as the indications for or against analysis, the just appraisal of which will influence the whole of the subsequent development of the treatment; nor on the introductory period, which consists of a few initial talks, usually two or three, during which the indications for psychoanalytic treatment are considered, and the general arrangements for the treatment are settled. The analyst is expected to maintain a prudent reserve, the very picture of that benevolent neutrality he is supposed to represent; as to the practical dispositions he should have towards what he is going to undertake, we know all about their strictness, their conventional (but not artificial) character, even that aseptic surgical coldness about which some scrupulous practitioners dream. It is against this background that the patient, lying down, is asked to submit to the fundamental rule of saying everything which occurs to him.

And so the first phase of the analysis properly so called is entered upon, all prudence and watchful expectancy; the analyst is waiting for the transference to establish itself and calls this the time of the floating transference. The patient, who senses what is expected of him, naturally directs operations; sometimes, duly warned of what will happen, he rushes like an indifferent comedian into a transference to order; or, more subtle, and floating between two currents, he may drown the fish in a flood of brilliant reasoning. But, apart from cases where analysis is contra-indicated, it is rare for our fish not to end up by nibbling at the hook of the transference; one day or another, tired of being cunning, he says in his own way: 'I have had enough; your turn.'

The analyst strikes: the second phase has started, the patient is undergoing his transference neurosis. This is the true field of psychoanalysis, the fruitful time, the moment of truth, and everything that can be said has already been said about this middle period during which the patient relives his former conflicts within the psychoanalytic situation, experiences love and hate, and allows his anxiety, his fantasies and his primitive desires to come to the surface. It is a difficult time, in which the patient's submerged ego-defences find a fresh support in the defence transference; it is also the time when the analyst, constantly pressed by his questioner, has to fight his own subjective inclinations and watch most carefully all that is called, for this reason, the counter-transference. He uses the weapon of interpretation, concentrating on the reality of the moment in order to restore to it its full value and its true meaning.

It is only the analyst's resolution of this crucial period of the transference neurosis which brings the treatment to its last phase, that of liquidation, which we shall not go into here.

Two sequences may be described, each approximating fairly closely to the internal rhythm of these two phases, which, however, in the variety of actual experience, does not accord exactly with any schematic formulation.

The more traditional of the two considers the effects of frustration; it is well known that this concept, although insufficiently defined, greatly influences the practitioner's behaviour. Freud thinks it best for the analysis to proceed as far as possible in an atmosphere of restraint and frustration (the patient knows what it costs him, for his own good). It is easy to see that this frustration gives rise to a certain resentment which, on account of its instinctive character, is called aggressiveness. But as it is difficult to satisfy one's aggressiveness, particularly when with the psychoanalyst, the impulse in question takes a regressive turn. This is the principle of the sequence: frustration—aggressiveness—regression.

M. Bouvet, in an article on the typical psychoanalytic treatment[1] which has already become a classic, describes another sequence which accounts for the characteristic rhythm of the analysis in a rather more subtle fashion. He first of all considers the principal obstacle encountered during

[1] *Encyclopédie médico-chirurgicale*, Psychiatrie, Vol. III, 37.812 A 10–A 40.

the treatment, the patient's attitude of resistance, due to the fact that he cannot stand up to the revelations which the progress of the treatment involves; faced with this obstacle, at first sight insurmountable, the patient sets off on a detour, but this detour itself is of such a kind as to constitute the transference (which in a certain sense includes everything irrational that goes on within the analytic relationship). The analyst tirelessly responds to this transference by interpretation, which is traditionally expected to bear more on the defensiveness itself than on its contents, and to work always from the more superficial to the more profound, the art of interpretation depending both on intelligence and on opportunity. And so, after a variable number of sequences, of the form resistance—transference—interpretation, corresponding to the number of foci of resistance, the subject comes to the point of seeing clearly the nub of his neurosis. In this way the work of interpretation strips the fundamental conflict of all the concentric layers which have been covering it up without managing either to neutralize it or resolve it.

Both these sequences show the cyclic character, apparently triple, of the fundamental analytic rhythm, which should progress in concentric fashion from the surface towards the depths.

If we then ask what is generally thought to constitute the progress of the treatment, we notice that analysis in its contemporary form is usually considered to bear exclusively on the ego. All the analytic work is directed to this region of the personality; the healthy part of the ego, in collaboration with the therapist, will progressively win over to its cause its own defaulting sectors. And so one co-operates with the rational ego, the observing subject, in the search for the altered part of itself, the object, which has got too closely associated with the id or oppressed by the superego. If it is remembered that analysis is a dynamic process aiming at bringing about a balance between the forces which constitute the neurotic personality, we can say, as good practitioners, and in unambiguous terms, that psychoanalysis has only one aim: 'to increase the power and reach of the ego', thus enabling it to establish a much greater control over the impulses of the id and to free itself rationally from the oppression of the superego. Bouvet, to whom we have frequently referred for this technical sketch, although elsewhere we have had occasion to criticize him, says, 'the goal to be reached is an enrichment of the ego in the double register of knowledge and of increase in energy.'[1]

But how, behind his ego, the necessary mask of the expert, are we going to discover the psychoanalyst himself, the man who often says nothing just because he does not know and has nothing to say? This is certainly not going to be easy, because nothing frightens him more, despite himself, than that clear technical light which can so very quickly be lighting up nothing but empty roads. And then, what good will it do? Today's reliable prescriptions, now empty and faded, were once a shining discovery; why compose new formulae which, in one sense, will be the less alive the more they are known, the clearer and more easily available they become? It is characteristic of a neurosis to present us with mummified formulae like this, and the analyst who has nothing with which to counter them but a plan and a technique will certainly be committing himself to an everlasting and sterile game of illusion.

To give an account of our experience is to try to describe something living without thereby crystallizing it.

Actually, the most difficult thing for the analyst to do is to keep alive. Because he is being tempted all the time, in the very exercise of his profession, by all the easy refuges of the mask, the mirror, the neutrality itself, all of them defences which would eventually dispense him—theoretically—from having to live at the rate of sixty minutes an hour. Yes, Freud was right, the psychoanalyst's calling is one of the tasks

[1] *L'Évolution Psychiatrique*, 1956, no. II, pp. 515-40.

impossible to man. It is good for the practitioner to know and remember this, because his work now takes its place in life quite naturally among the other kinds of work. But this place has to be maintained; despite the misleading appearance of one's professional equipment, one cannot really install an armchair. What can one see from an armchair?

My clearest impression is of what happens at the beginning, when I decide to undertake a new case. A bond comes into existence, an engagement is entered into. On one side the patient agrees to come and talk to me at regular intervals over a period of time the length of which is as uncertain to him as it is to me. I agree, on my side, to accept responsibility for him, however bored I may eventually get; I engage myself to listen to him—more, if possible to understand him. If I do not altogether know what is in store for me, he knows even less; he is deceiving himself already in affirming the purity and firmness of his desire to be cured, an affirmation, however, which is practically essential. What he wants is somebody to accept responsibility for him, or perhaps he wants an excuse (I shall have done everything I should), or else he hopes to make himself loved. But whatever it is, he is partly ignorant (without knowing it) of the true motive behind his engagement. But, without being taken in, and sizing up in my own way, as far as may be, the nature and strength of his true motivation, I make myself for all practical purposes, and in his eyes, the accomplice of his self-deception; I accept his engagement, and knot the thread of the analysis, which in this way starts off with the double seal of the deception and the bond. That is to say—and up to this point I can describe what happens without difficulty—at least I recognize him as capable of making and keeping a compact; I recognize in him from the beginning, despite the fact that he is bogged down in his own imaginary good reasons, this necessary minimum of openness to the symbolic order, to those things, that is to say, which are the foundation of compacts, bonds and laws. Then I put before him the law which is to govern our dialogue, the paradoxical law of talking freely.

I think (but perhaps it is just that this is the time I know best) that it is the beginning that is the vital part of our joint experience, giving it its particular constitution and marking with its own characteristic quality the deep-set rhythm of the analysis; for there is never any end to the light that can be thrown on what it was that happened at that inaugural moment to constitute this self-deception and forge this bond.

There are certainly other aspects of the analysis about which I ought to have some sort of knowledge, but they are a bit vague in my mind, and my memories concerning them are dim and fleeting, and I can only offer one or two very short fragments of themes which should perhaps find a place in the rhythm I am supposed to be scanning. I should first like to suggest that the quasi-obsessional rite which rules the timetable and the rhythm of the sessions during a period of time indefinite of its very nature constitutes an aspect of the dynamics of the treatment which, although generally accepted, is not very well understood. Then I also think that the psychoanalytic history, as it gradually unfolds, is not at all like a jig-saw puzzle, to be reconstituted by finding the missing pieces; what really matters is the history constituted today by the subject's conversation: so that when a patient recounts the 'fact' of his younger brother's birth, the history is quite different according to whether he says: 'my little brother was born when I had been sent on holiday to my aunt's' or: 'my brother Jacques was born during the holidays while I was staying with my aunt.'

All things considered, I have nothing more to say on these two subjects beyond these brief references, but I am sorry and offer my apologies.

I will now turn to another essential period of the analysis, and should like to talk about the interpretation.

In this completely unbalanced dialogue which we call psychoanalysis, the interpretation comes in as the therapist's contribution. However infrequent it may be, it is this that constitutes the analysis as a dialogue. How, then, does it work, and what is its value and efficacity? This is certainly a fundamental question, whatever theoretical view may be held regarding psychoanalysis, because everyone will agree in recognizing in the interpretation the specific action of the psychoanalytic process.

Let us recall the principal elements of the situation: the patient, bound to the therapist by an engagement, tries as he talks to observe the law of sincerity and freedom. So his discourse, by its very nature a question, is always waiting for an answer which it does not get, or at least it does not get the answer it wants. More often than not he receives nothing in return for his words, apart from the habitual silence, except interpretations which seem to him at first sight to be nothing but asides. The action is woven round this curious dialogue: hope, deception, resentment, perplexity, announce the emotional storms which will facilitate the transference.

An example will help me better than anything else to give some idea of the period of interpretation, although it must be understood that any practitioner would be able in all charity to say that it is a bad one, ill chosen, perhaps too fragmentary.

The patient, a typical obsessive, is talking fluently, quite at ease in this dialogue which he would like to turn into an intimate chat (rather like another patient who remarked quite sincerely: 'it seems to me that I am spending my time bearing the brunt of the conversation for you, so as to keep it nicely going'.) This first patient said: 'I like coming here so long as I am not forced to go too fast, and I feel quite at ease with you; you don't speak very often, I know, but I am used to that; and then sometimes, when you do happen to open your mouth, it is like a firework (*feu d'artifice*), but unfortunately you always fall back into a relapse.'

I intervene: 'What is artificial?'

'Oh, there you go again.' He takes me up in the manner of a speaker accustomed to dealing with every eventuality. But today 'artificial' does not get us anywhere; he changes his tone, he remembers his passionate taste for the theatre, goes back to his old obsession with fire, literally brings his own mouth into play (I cannot go into detail) and eventually accuses the analyst of being completely artificial, which gives me the opportunity to intervene again and say: 'no, conventional' (verbal, or 'oral' of course).

I offer you this fragment, which is rather heavily cut. The interpretation here is then literally 'what is artificial?' which is in the form of a question.

I ought, in the first place, to be able to explain how this interpretation arose. I will avoid entrenching myself technically behind intuition or my own unconscious. As a matter of fact, I was struck by the metaphor he used and flattered by it, because it made me sound a brilliant conversationalist, just like himself; and he spoke to me personally, which could be understood as a manifestation of the transference. But I have been taught to listen with a neutral ear, whether the remarks are flattering or hostile, and to give equal attention to all the points of a discourse, and so I picked up the word 'fire', which in the elegant language my patient sees fit to use (it is an affectation, anyway) put me in mind of his frustrated passions just as much as of his old obsession with fire. I then drew attention to 'artificial' because I always try to follow M. Lacan's teaching and distinguish the imagery which is called up in me by a word (in this case 'artificial')[1] from symbolism (why should not fire be regarded as the bond *par excellence?*) Besides, I knew of his taste for the theatre and for décor, about which he had often talked in order to show me that his father had never understood him. Finally I knew (I nearly said, as well as he did) that this sort of conversation is a feint, a protection, and also a call for help. And so I intervened, in order by means of a question to bring home to him the use he was making, as a defence but also as a question, of the figure of the empty talker who pours tepid water out of his mouth (is it to be more sure of putting out the fire?)

[1] The imagery would be that of a firework, *'feu d'artifice'*. – Tr.

But the practitioner in me wakes up and asks: 'is your interpretation correct?' For a moment I am troubled, then I tell him: 'I don't really know.' The interpretation was the one that came to me, in a moment, in the way I have just explained; I do not think it is false, by which I mean that it answers a question, indicates the transference, points out an obstacle, and offers an opening; but I am quite sure that in an exactly similar context someone else would have intervened differently or not at all (as I myself might have acted differently if the time of the session or my mood had been different). I am tempted to say, what does it matter? After all, I said something, I interpreted with those few brief words; but it remains essential, I think, to be able to give as complete an account as possible of the meaning, motivation and intention of this intervention.

It is more difficult to examine with perfect objectivity the effect that these words had on my questioner. In the first place he just took them into the framework of friendly chatter: 'Oh, there you go again', but soon there is a break; his tone changes, becomes more hesitant, less assured; memories which, if they did not rise up into consciousness as fresh discoveries, were at least newly associated, at least by contiguity, were brought up again. Finally he protests, relying on a word which betrays him, ready, too ready perhaps, to allow himself to be persuaded (I was going to say robbed). But it would be necessary to give the subsequent course of his conversation at much greater length to show exactly how its course had been changed by the interpretation.

This can be shown more simply by a brief example, taken from the associations in a dream of a woman patient; doubtless, as you will see, this new example has come to my mind by way of association with this significant word 'fire'—which is itself worthy of analysis. This patient dreamed of a beautiful bird, which suddenly appeared at her side, looking like a bird made of felt (*un oiseau fait de feutre*), and began talking to her of inconsequential trifles. I intervened to say 'Firebird', (*oiseau de feu*) and we then talked about this ballet, of which she was very fond, and excerpts of which she had once taken part in, although at that time I did not know.

The best way to express my idea of what the action of interpretation signifies is to say that it marks time, scanning the internal rhythm of the analysis. Fresh evidence of the living presence of the analyst (and we all know how the patient comes to doubt this), it constitutes under a new mode, that of the present moment, a commentary on the original bond; like a pivot, it is the centre of a movement which it itself sets going. The wording of the interpretation does not suggest a translation (because it does not link up with anything already established) so much as a conversion, in the dynamic sense of the term; by turning the word round it presents it from another point of view, so that the defensive word, detention, is shown as de-tension[1] and the verbal similarity is made the basis of a meaningful question...

Ought I to apologize for leaving everything in the air at this point? It is rather like the end of an analysis, which the patient one day discovers is not really the end of anything, but only, after all, an opening and another beginning.

---

[1] This is a literal example which was 'offered' (I may say) for my interpretation by the patient mentioned in the first example.

FREUD AND THE
ANALYTIC SCHOOLS

CAN ONE TALK ABOUT
PSYCHOANALYTIC ORTHODOXY?

Dr Vladimir Granoff

To hear the experts talk one would think it was not in question. It is talked about. In fact nothing else is talked about.
A traditional psychoanalyst, an orthodox psychoanalyst, no,
he is not very orthodox, etc. What, then, is this doctrine by
reference to which it is so easy to distinguish those who are
orthodox from those who are not? What are the criteria for
such apparently conclusive statements? We shall also have
to investigate the approach of those people who weigh up,
judge and classify in this manner.

Let us try, if only to be ready to modify our opinion, not
to be on our guard and not to hide our surprise, so that we
feel the same surprise that anyone else would feel, initiated
or not. How then can such a question, with its train of
frightening consequences, come to be asked in psychoanalysis, where nothing but cool reasoning should reign, where,
as in every science, a scientifically objective atmosphere of
discussion should always prevail?

Has not psychoanalysis acquired rights of citizenship in the
medicine of today? It no longer counts its successes and
doctors trust their patients to it in every increasing numbers.
It has long ago lost that disquieting halo of ambiguous novelty. The body of psychoanalysts is solidly organized. Why
then this unleashing of passions?

At first sight it would seem natural for things to take the
same course in psychoanalysis as they do in the medical

sciences. Complete agreement is rare in those sciences, as it is anywhere else. Opinion is divided among various theories. These theories are often simply divergent, although sometimes they are contradictory. One judges according to the facts, or suspends judgement while waiting for the facts to emerge. Proof is provided by the results of treatment, by development, by laboratory experiments. One waits for an adequate statistical perspective. And since in psychoanalysis also there are successes and failures it is not easy to see why the same discipline should not regulate the discussion.

If one looks a little more closely, however, it is immediately seen that even in medicine controversies reach the point at which interdicts are pronounced, and the more recent history of medicine, at the dawn of the age of Pasteur, shows to what extremes men of science are often carried. This example is characteristic, because the same recurring factor can be found on all these occasions. A strong personality around which passions are unleashed, for or against.

This is just the case with psychoanalysis. For when it is said of a psychoanalyst that he is orthodox, it is Freudian orthodoxy that is meant.

It is only necessary to look at the different fate of the terms 'traditional' and 'orthodox' in psychoanalysis. Most writers, quite rightly, hesitate to make use of the idea of tradition in relation to a practice so recent and so varied, but no one seems to find it embarrassing to pass judgement on the degree of orthodoxy of treatment, writings, or persons, because they are judging in accordance with Freud's teaching, as they understand it through their own study, or, more often, through what they have been taught. And so there will be sects, even a church. One may question the idea of belonging to an orthodoxy in the field in question, as being the adoption in its totality of an original doctrine worked out by one man, but it follows from the application of this idea that there may even be heresies in this field.

Is this the case? Since orthodoxy always goes hand in hand

with the idea that doctrine may not be altered, which is what guarantees its validity, heresy cannot be regarded as a minor difference or as an imperfection. On the contrary, it will be regarded as a perversion of the doctrine. And so completely lost. Is it possible that this is the case here, if not *de jure* then at least *de facto*? And if so, in relation to what truth?

Before trying to answer these questions, always supposing that it is going to be possible to give an unqualified answer, it is necessary to take a look at what is in fact taking place among psychoanalysts themselves.

There at least we might expect to find some light and some straightforward data to go on. Because, once the ducks' eggs had been thrown out of the nest, or had fallen out on their own, which happened during Freud's life-time, Freudian psychoanalysts may be regarded as having stayed together. The stability of their institutions, always increasing in size and complexity, should inspire confidence.

But the subjects of their discussions, together with the instances that make the law, as well as day to day experience, all point to the existence of serious disagreement, the noise of which penetrates the walls which they have built in vain around the places where the discussions are held. Some of this noise still echoes in many ears throughout France. And if one turns to the history of the psychoanalytic movement it will be seen that, apart from the major schisms, it has always been like this. Only with this difference, that during the founder's life-time recourse to him personally was always possible. The whole meaning of the situation turns on whether he is available or not.

Because, in fact, the problem of Freudian orthodoxy properly speaking did not appear until the day after Freud's death. While he was alive one should rather speak of Freudian obedience. In order for it to be possible to invoke the name of Freud as it is invoked today, it was necessary first that Freud should die. Today interdicts are hurled in his name, anathemas are pronounced, dismissals decided upon. In his name some particular teaching is declared wrong and the teachers lacking in faith and authority. If circumstances permit they are deprived of the right to practise. Here again we see the irreducible difference separating this discipline from that of medicine.

Medical practitioners may be suspended, but it is usually for breaches of discipline in the strict sense of the word and not for offences against an orthodoxy.

In order to understand this state of affairs it is necessary to turn to the history of the movement. There is no question here of looking at it as a whole: only one facet needs considering.

It was Freud, and Freud alone, who invented psychoanalysis. He alone has brought it to the stage of development we know today and he alone remains responsible for its orientation as a whole. There is no need here to emphasize the radically novel character of his discovery, as this has already been done by other writers. It is enough to say that if his theory has its roots in the scientific knowledge of its time, it nevertheless differs from it as much as the flower differs from the bulb from which it springs, and that its revolutionary implications make it one of the most complete and authentic adventures of the human mind.

Looked at from the outside its development seems to ramble; the inflexible line of its progress is not seen until Freud's work is studied. This work saw the light of day in a hostile climate and succeeded in provoking a united opposition. An iron will and unparalleled obstinacy were necessary in order to persevere. To be one of his disciples certainly needed courage and a great deal of confidence in Freud personally and devotion to him. A comparison with the commandoes is not out of place.

And it is known that Freud himself did not always manage to resist the romantic attraction of this heroic position. The dream of a brotherhood united by a secret pact was bound to come to nothing, but it is worth remembering that it was

Freud who thought of it, and not as a game; he was past the age for games. And so the progress of psychoanalysis in its heroic period was never unattended by passion.

Psychoanalysis, as can be seen very clearly from its history, took shape partly as a result of the elaboration of Freud's teaching, and partly as a result of the more or less turbulent adhesion of his pupils to the work of their master. Eventually Freud more or less adopted an attitude of withdrawal from public debate. One cannot avoid the impression that if Freud regarded himself as the guardian of his own discovery, he also regarded it as inevitable that battles should rage about it in an atmosphere of comparative misunderstanding of his work. Freud's genius cannot be said ever to have been completely unveiled. A feeling persists that he has not said his last word.

This was enough to keep his followers in relative uncertainty, and to give rise to all sorts of diverse interpretations. And so one sees the leaders of the movement taking up positions sometimes quite different from each other, but each on the basis of his personal knowledge of Freud.

The situation is further complicated by the fact that Freud's writings are of all writings the most paradoxical, and so lend themselves admirably to exegesis. Some find his writing characterized by a limpid clarity, and regard conflicting passages as being ultimately not analysable, to be disregarded for the sake of simplicity and for practical purposes. For others, more prudent or more respectful, the very unity of the work resides in this paradox, and nothing can be cut out without spoiling the whole.

It is in the most difficult passages, which are sometimes described as speculative, in the pejorative sense of the word, that they find the keystone of the whole edifice. A failure to appreciate the paradox completely extinguishes the right to understand any of Freud's work whatsoever. And it should be borne in mind that opinions are completely divided on the cardinal problem referred to as that of instinctual fusion.

No combination of circumstances would seem at first sight more unsuitable as a basis for radical judgements about the doctrinal orientation of psychoanalysts. But in fact the opposite seems to be the case.

It is only by trying to understand the situation by means of the bias of the analytic method itself that one can get anywhere near to explaining it.

In relation to psychoanalysis Freud has occupied, and still occupies, a position which nobody has ever thought of challenging. Let us set this element of the problem down as part of the initial data and let us suppose for the moment, for the sake of the argument, that nothing has since come along to make us alter this proposition. It follows that any appeal to Freudian arbitration, during his lifetime, was an appeal to something that Freud might say but had not yet said. Since his death to invoke his name is to appeal to something which he has not said, might have said, but now never will. And so he can be made to say whatever you like. What we have here is, *mutatis mutandis*, not very different from the Freudian superego itself, which says precisely nothing, which is what it is meant do do. And to those who make use of Freud's absence as a factor in the situation in this way, it may be said that many elements of Freud's teaching do not really say anything much.

Can we pass judgement on this state of affairs? Could it have been avoided? Possibly. But it is difficult to see how.

Psychoanalysis is not reducible to any existing medical discipline, and it is permeated by a philosophy which is not easy to grasp.

Without this philosophy, psychoanalysis is unapproachable and incomprehensible. However, since it is a branch of medicine, its name figures in the list of those sciences which until recently, and even sometimes today, openly pride themselves, if we may use this expression, on keeping clear of philosophy. It is also from among the doctors that psychoanalysis has recruited most of its practitioners. Moreover, to such an extent does the stature of its founder seem to surpass that of his pupils, and the reach of his message the comprehension of his successors, that it is hardly to be wondered at that Freud expressed himself as pessimistic with regard to the quality of the personnel of the movement or at the fact that psychoanalysts always have to return to his work, which in any case has certainly not yet disclosed all its riches. And then his very style, although of a masterly precision and clarity, is keyed to the particular cadence of his teaching, and effectively prevents that facile optimism which a superficial reading might have engendered. As soon as elements are acquired they are immediately put in motion, and everything is all the time kept in vital and perpetual movement, which does not exactly provide the mind with a quiet and comfortable basis for reflection. We may adapt a saying of Dante's and say of those who are thinking of entering on the study of psychoanalysis, that they should leave all desire for comfort on the threshold.

There is no doubt that this situation has provided its own remedy, both on the level of Freud's significance as a superego and on that of the comfortless philosophy of his teaching. The question is rather to know whether the remedy is not worse than the evil. It is only too clear that the complication only exists to the extent that one resigns onself to it. And also certain modern currents of thought have decided to simplify, to the point of creating a psychoanalysis that could be called aerodynamic. As to Freud's authority, it is in fact rejected on the controversial points, although to all appearances safeguarded with regard to everything else. The appeal to Freud then becomes purely formal, and equivalent to the English expression 'lip-service'. The mouth pronounces words that the mind doesn't think. In this way, by means of additions and subtractions, a neo-Freudian doctrine takes shape. All the appearances being in this way safeguarded, it will lay claim to a strict Freudian orthodoxy. This doctrinal neoformation is psychoanalytically a characteristic growth of our time.

Is this as much as to say that, in the light of these results, the very idea of psychoanalytic orthodoxy should be rejected en bloc, as an inconvenient burden with disastrous consequences? By no means. Freud himself saw the results, sometimes unfortunate, brought about even during his life-time by the expansion of psychoanalysis and the organization of its institutions. He opposed this, often with anger, but in the end with a certain dignity, as if he had eventually developed a detachment with regard to this creature which had been born of his mind. This attitude on the part of a man who remained creative right to the end cannot be explained by age nor by the illness which overtook him towards the end of his days. It would seem rather that in the event he was motivated by a sort of resignation at not being able to control this thing, which, once made public, had escaped from his power. And perhaps this austerity of feeling was, taken all in all, a lesser evil, guaranteeing his work against a complete dilution, of which there were signs even during his life-time, against an abandonment of all discipline, in theory and practice, and echoing those very psychological conflicts from the study of which psychoanalysis was born.

It may be difficult to say who keeps to this orthodoxy, and to say where it is to be found and where it is not, apart, of course, from those elaborations in which the essentials of the Freudian doctrine have been discarded, but it is possible to state that it must necessarily be somewhere and that it is perhaps in this very clash of contradictions that it is actually to be found.

From the difficulty of defining it we may at least conclude with some certainty where it is not to be found. In no circumstances can this Freudian orthodoxy be reduced to its formal aspect, either on the theoretical or on the practical level.

Some of the points of reference of Freud's teaching are analytic, and some are beyond psychoanalysis altogether. And it must not be forgotten that if these latter bear the imprint of their time, the former refer to a science only in its infancy, not completely developed, and, as such, in constant movement.

The points of reference which are beyond psychoanalysis are inevitably affected by the particular stage reached in the development of science and contemporary thought. Permanence and exclusiveness with regard to the internal references in the field of psychoanalysis in the strict sense cannot be a pledge of doctrinal solidity, because that would be to make of it a closed circuit and to regard psychoanalysis as a completed doctrine. Nothing could be more opposed to Freud's own approach and the continual state of movement to which everything was submitted by him. Such an untroubled Freudianism would do nothing but draw the fruit of tranquillity from the failure to define its premises.

No more can Freudian orthodoxy be reduced to a standardization of technique. Freud has given us sufficient warning to this effect. If a certain superficial resemblance in procedure may be observed throughout psychoanalytic practice this is due to the particular nature of the dialogue. Beyond this, each one takes part in it in his own way. And those enquiries which have been sharp enough to pierce the wall of reticence give evidence of considerable divergence. Neither the shape of the couch nor the colour of the armchair can be taken as an identification mark. Nor any codification made by those pernickety minds which will only, the next day, be found evading the demands of the codification it had pleased them to make the day before.

Instead of taking a bird's-eye view and trying to set a typical analysis and its constituent parts up as a yardstick, one should proceed in the reverse order, and take as an indication of Freudian orthodoxy whatever in Freud's work is the least easily defined, circumscribed, labelled and catalogued. His spirit, in all its fullness. In a word, his style. Rich, compressed to the point of being dense, certainly, but airy and open. First cut the barbed wire. Afterwards the broad view, the panorama, but only afterwards. In order to discover in the very centre of the field of vision that to follow Freud is to guarantee psychoanalysis against all the traps set for it by fanatics.

And in the first place the trap which tries to make it overstep its limits, while preventing it from properly exploring the area within those limits. Analysis is not a world system and does not provide an explanation of the world, any more than it leads to a better future. It is not a social therapy. It is not a re-adjustment exercise. There is nothing in it to support a cool optimism which might provide psychoanalysts with an alibi or an excuse to segregate themselves.

It is nothing but an arduous meditation, continually being re-thought, upon what its subjects have said. An ear open to those words which they address beyond the armchair to someone who is not there. Talking and keeping silent, by both of which the words of the subject find their place in the universal conversation. That is the mainspring of the treatment. Freud himself has warned us that it cannot cure everyone.

THE DOCTRINE OF ADLER

Andrée Hauser

The study of analysis and of its development is not complete without an account of Alfred Adler's Individual Psychology, itself derived from psychopathology.

Alfred Adler (1870–1937) a Viennese physician contemporary with Freud, based his method on certain fundamental concepts which rapidly led to his separation from him. The position taken up by Freud and his circle with regard to sexuality led to a definite break between the two thinkers and to the development of two different streams of thought.

In 1907 Adler published a monograph, *A Study of Organic Inferiority and its Psychical Compensation*[1]; he based his study on a biological conception of human nature, and drew attention to what was to be an essential point in his psychology, the unity of the personality. It is this concept that gives his psychology its name, and confusion can be caused if the term is not understood in its etymological sense, *individere;* he says it is not possible to divide the individual. And so he regarded the human person as being in the first place a complex of organic and psychological functions in a state of perpetual becoming, and inseparable from those other higher unities by which he is surrounded, family, social group, society, cosmos.

This idea of unity takes on its full value and all its originality from the moment Adler relates it to that of purpose.

[1] New York, 1917.

He was not satisfied with the idea of causality, which for him constituted only one aspect of the problem, but was more concerned with the dynamism of the individual, and introduced the idea of a final cause, to account for the creative activity of the individual, directed to a goal which transcends him. Individual Psychology is one of the first existential psychologies. It offers man the hope of freeing himself from the sense of fatalism.

Adler's theory is completed by his *Gemeinschaftsgefühl*, or *Social Interest*.[1] On account of his initial weakness, man must live in society. Social interest is higher than social feeling, which is a simple necessity depending on the instinct of self-preservation. It is a guiding aim, by means of which a man develops his potentialities. As he goes on towards the fulfilment of his own personality, in a social direction, a man realizes himself and finds his balance. This enables Adler to say that Individual Psychology is 'probably the most consistent theory of the position of the individual with regard to the problems of social living and is in this sense, therefore, a social psychology.'[2]

Inferiority Feeling and Psychological Compensation

As a specialist in constitutional pathology, Adler took the study of organ inferiority as the starting point of his research. At a time when medicine was much concerned with the study of microbial disease on account of Pasteur's discoveries, Adler turned his interest to the subject attacked by the disease, and particularly to its localization and the possibility of the individual being predisposed to vulnerability at a particular point. He concluded that it was not the disease that was hereditary but the underlying organic inferiority.

---

[1] London, 1938.
[2] *Individualpsychologie in der Schule*, Leipzig, 1929, p. 108. H. & L. Ansbacher, ed. *The Individual Psychology of Alfred Adler: a Systematic Presentation in Selections from His Writing*, Allen & Unwin, 1958, p. 157.

From the biological point of view each cell and each organ contains within itself for the purpose of its own conservation the means of compensating, and sometimes of over-compensating, for an inferiority. If the skin is cut or burned this provokes a proliferation of cicatrical cells, so that the tissue is repaired. A broken bone which has reknit often has a more resistant callus than the original bone. The removal of a kidney results in the other working harder to re-establish the equilibrium. Further, since each organ exists in terms of the functioning of the whole, the different systems of the human body work together; the brain plays the role of compensating organ even more than that of co-ordinating organ. When there is some organic defect the deficient organ stimulates the central nervous system and provokes psychological compensation.

Adler was the first to point out the fact, now regarded as classic, that there are musicians like Beethoven who have hearing troubles, painters like Manet who have something wrong with their vision and lawyers and orators who have suffered from speech defects. This is not so much compensation as over-compensation, since the individual has managed, by means of courage and effort, to turn his defect into an asset. The important thing to notice is the subjective interpretation which different people put on the same weakness. One left-handed person may use his clumsiness as an excuse for his failures, in his own eyes and in those of others, while another may take a contrary line and put all his energy into compensating for his original defect. Adler says that 'it matters little what we bring with us into the world, everything depends on what we do with it.'[1]

In the case of normal children an inferiority feeling is not based on a mistake or a defect, but is related to the situation of inferiority in which the human infant remains for so many months. If a baby develops an inferiority feeling on account

[1] M. Ganz, *The Psychology of Alfred Adler and the Development of the Child*, London, 1953, p. 10.

of this situation he may later use it as an excuse and as an obstacle to development.

By the system of compensation the child tries to escape from the feeling of insecurity which results from the inferiority feeling by inventing a fictitious future for his own reassurance. 'When I am... if I were...' In order to escape from the inferiority feeling the human person needs to lean on a fiction which springs up all the more forcefully the more overwhelming is the feeling of organic inferiority experienced by the child: it is the desire for security which creates the ideal of personality, which is a synthesis of all the gifts and all the possibilities of which the child feels himself to be frustrated. According to the German philosopher, Vaihinger, from whom Adler borrowed this idea, this guiding fiction corresponds to a human need to make use of hypotheses to account for everything in the world which is unorganized. The hypotheses provide a number of points of reference, which are artificial, but serve to reassure and orientate him; for example, scientific hypotheses providing a basis for future research, classifications and typology, geographical divisions of the globe, etc. For Individual Psychology the guiding fiction of the 'as if...' is organized around criteria based on evaluations which may be true or false, according to the subject. A person's whole attitude is directed towards one single end, to square the ideal with reality. 'No matter from what angle we observe the psychic development of a normal or neurotic person he is always found ensnared in the meshes of his particular fiction; a fiction from which the neurotic is unable to find his way back to reality and in which he believes while the normal person utilizes it for the purpose of reaching a definite goal.'[1]

To reach this end the individual adopts a style of life, acquired by a process of trial and error; this represents for him the attitude which he thinks, rightly or wrongly, to be

[1] Adler, *The Neurotic Constitution*, Routledge and Kegan Paul, 1921, p. 18; R. & H. Ansbacher, *op. cit.*, p. 96.

the most effective one for getting what he wants, which is power, for the sake of his own security. Adler allots a vital place to the will to power, as the determining and creative principle in the formation and even in the nature of the ideal of the personality.

Formation of the Life-Style

If the life-style of the child depends in the first place on his evaluation of his own body and of his hereditary constitution, it is also moulded from birth onwards by the reactions and demands of his surroundings. The environment intervenes to make the child adapt himself and master his functions.

The first person to intervene is the mother. It is through her personality, her love or her rejection, her calmness or her anxiety, her orderliness or her confusion, that the child will draw his first conclusions regarding the world around him. She forms with him his first link in the social chain, and upon this first relationship will depend to a large extent his attitude of trust or distrust towards the world. In order to prevent this relationship becoming an exclusive one, the mother should take care to direct the child's interest towards his father, his brothers and sisters, and eventually society in general.

The father does not figure so much in these early contacts and appears in the eyes of the child as the one who wields the authority. If his personality is balanced he may provide the child with his masculine ideal. It is generally the father who has more contact with the outside world, and makes the bridge between the family circle and the wider society. Through his personality and his personal achievements the child will get his first impression of work and vocation.

As well as the parents there are the children, forming with them, according to the Adlerian expression, a family constellation. From the point of view of each of these stars, the constellation as a whole will have a different perspective.

The variation in character between different children in one family depends to a great extent on their personal view, and this variation is repeated so consistently in all families that it is possible to describe certain types, corresponding to the original situation in the family.

The character of the eldest is influenced by the fact that for a certain time he was the sole focus of his parents' love and attention. A certain flavour of bitterness and disillusionment often permeates throughout life the attitude of eldest children. In many cases they turn their affection away from the mother, whose preoccupation with the newcomer disappoints them, and attach themselves to the father. They often tend to support authority and exaggerate the importance of laws and rules. Everything should be done by rule and they will maintain a conservative attitude throughout life. They acquire quite young a sense of their own responsibility, often excessive, which extends to their younger brothers and beyond the family.

The type of the second child is in marked contrast. He lives in the future. He looks forward to the time when he will be able to catch up with the eldest, or even to pass him. If the eldest is the traditionalist, the second in the family is the revolutionary. The youngest child, on account of the principle of compensation, hopes to become the head of the family, particularly if he is crushed by the older children and deeply discouraged by this fact.

The only child is used to living with adults and is often afraid to venture beyond the family circle. He may try to play a role in order to retain his privileged place. If he does not learn to make a real effort he will content himself by being unique, but in some inessential and useless way.

It is not intended by means of these character sketches to force everyone into a rigid classification, which would be quite foreign to the spirit of Adlerian psychology. They are just intended to give some idea of how the formation of character can be affected by the position in the family.

Every psychology seeks to understand the human person in terms of his heredity and his environment, putting the accent more particularly on one or other of these factors. Adler, with his constructive optimism, refused to allow himself to regard the personality as determined only by heredity and environment. For him the third constructive element is the child himself, 'the artist of his own personality.'[1]

The interpretation of life which each person works out for himself, and which constitutes the basis of his life-style, is not formulated in words or expressed in concepts, but during the first four or five years of life the child has already directed his efforts towards a particular end, and established a basic relationship between his body and mind. At the end of this time his own particular style has been adopted, with its corresponding emotional and psychological habits. As the individual is a unity, the consistency of his style of life is shown in his bodily stances, his mimicry, his behaviour, his way of doing things, of feeling, of willing, his interpretation of facts, his selection of memories, his dreams. What we take to be contradictions in the manifestation of a personality are easily explained once we have understood the life-style and the aim which the individual has fixed for himself, consciously or unconsciously. What may have looked in the first place like a contradiction in his behaviour or character is only a question of different tactics.

This disposition which the individual acquires, which is added to and perfected by each of his impressions and experiences, and which conditions his every perception, Adler calls a scheme of apperception.

The Problem of Adaptation

From the sociological point of view which Adler takes, a man is seen as an individual who lives in society; if he is normal, he has enough courage and energy to meet the difficulties of

[1] Adler, *The Education of Children*, Allen & Unwin, 1930, p. 5.

social life as they come along. If he is maladjusted he shrinks from social demands. For Adler all the problems of life are subordinated to the problems of social life (comradeship), the relationship between the sexes (love and marriage) and work (profession, occupation). They do not arise from our instincts, but present themselves in terms of our human situation, with its concrete difficulties of life in a community.

A satisfactory adaptation gives the individual the satisfaction of being well-balanced in himself, and also the knowledge that society derives a certain advantage from his work. Faulty adjustment results in the child's training himself in a direction which is socially useless, possibly to the extent of a neurosis, and puts an unbridgeable abyss between him and other people.

As long as a child is training himself towards socially useful forms of compensation for his weakness he is fitting himself to cope with the demands of life and is on the road to correct adaptation. Each point successfully reached is for him an achievement which brings with it the courage to make a further advance. But suppose the child does not persevere in his training, and does not make progress. His sense of inferiority will remain uncompensated and will halt his efforts and lessen the future chances of success. Between himself and the superiority which is his goal there opens up a gulf of anxiety and discouragement.

Adler distinguishes three kinds of children in whom this failure in adaptive training may occur, those with defective organs, those who are pampered, and those who are neglected.

As we have already seen, the demands of the environment bear heavily on an organism handicapped at the start by defective organs. A greater effort of compensation is necessary then, and it is interesting to see how the family can intelligently help the child to make progress in such a case by allowing him to experiment, while making sure that what he is trying to do is proportionate to his capacity; on the other hand the family can make things more difficult for him by discouraging his tentative efforts.

The pampered child, being by definition the centre of interest for his family, will be very much at a loss as soon as he loses his privileged position. He has been trained to expect and not to give. He has never had the opportunity of acquiring independence and does not know how to do anything by himself. His attitude is one of always looking for protection.

The third category covers those deprived children who have never known what it is to be surrounded by encouragement and love. On account of this unfortunate situation they have acquired the habit of over-rating the problems of life and under-rating their own capacity to meet them. Such children feel their isolated and difficult position as something they cannot get out of by themselves. They have never had the opportunity of stepping out into life with confidence in themselves and in other people.

These types of maladjustment result in a child's being caught in a vicious circle. The more keenly he feels his own incapacity when faced with test situations such as starting school, being compared with other people, etc., the more strongly and tensely will he seek success of any sort to give himself the illusion of superiority. So begins a fantasy of unattainable greatness, which still further increases the distance between imagination and reality, and may well lead to neurosis.

The pampered child, like the neurotic one, soon turns away from the path of normal development, which has always led to failure. He learns to make use of the weakness itself, and feels the need to hide it by sheltering behind those adults who seem so strong and whom he also dominates by attaching himself to them personally. He buries himself in his own idea of his weakness, in anxiety, timidity and domination.

According to Adler, the various problems of life are related to the conditions under which human beings live on this earth, and to the more or less favourable responses which they need to make. For the survival of the species man has to live with other people, and rely on their reactions, and he must adapt himself to social life and be interested in his neighbours in order to understand them. The best situation from which to respond to these pressures is an attitude of friendliness, social feeling and co-operation. It was the discovery of the importance of co-operation which made possible the division of labour and consequent increase in production.

Without discussing in detail the vast fields of friendship and work it is important to point out that those people who evade their problems and refuse to co-operate are a heavy burden on those who are actively engaged in the struggle for life. None of these problems can be considered separately because each for its resolution requires a favourable attitude towards the others.

Sex: Love and Marriage

In order to understand Adler's position with regard to sex it is necessary to take account of social ideas regarding the role of man and woman. Despite a steady improvement in the position of women from the beginning of this century, it is none the less true that the norms according to which we live are still based on a scale of values fixed by a certain type of civilization—the patriarchal. The desire for power on the part of various people and various classes has led, throughout history, to the masculine sex having the preponderate importance. This tendency has given rise to an antithetic value judgement which refers all the strong characteristics to the masculine sex and all weakness to the feminine. For human beings living in a world where the man dominates the woman the mechanism of the inferiority feeling and its psychological compensation easily explain the tension which upsets the harmony between the sexes.

A boy who develops harmoniously will follow from choice

the path which opens in front of him, strewn with masculine privilege. One who shows difficulties in adapting himself will seek his personality ideal in an exaggerated affirmation of his masculinity: violence rather than strength, and exaggerated sexuality. And so his desire for superiority will express itself in seeking to dominate and to be a 'real' man.

The 'masculine protest' in a woman is an attitude of revolt, arising from her dissatisfaction with her feminine role. The psychological life of a woman shows the same dispositions as that of any human being who finds himself in a position of inferiority and unable to alter this intolerable situation.

In their opposition, some women seek to remedy their inferior position by a masculine attitude. Taking an active line they make every effort to surpass the young people around them, seeking in their occupation and their amusements those which are more suited to the male sex. Developing in this way along masculine lines, the masculine protest can go so far as to give rise to psycho-somatic troubles which are really a refusal of femininity, marriage and motherhood.

Other women go through life with such a marked attitude of resignation, docility and humility as to suggest some underlying significance. Their self-control and the state of tension arising from the perpetual effort to suppress their revolt often betray themselves by nervous or psycho-somatic troubles similar to those found in the masculine type of woman.

In some cases, where there has been a positive adaptation and well-directed energy, the masculine protest has led to personal achievement.

Sexuality is awakened and stimulated prematurely in either sex whenever there is a strong feeling of inferiority with a conscious masculine protest as compensation. The individual either uses his sexuality to reassure himself with regard to his own power, or else he gets rid of it and depreciates it, according to his particular tendency. Adler says that everyone has the sexuality he deserves. The sexual impulse is not a cause of action, but rather a means of arriving at a

goal. It is a symbol which expresses the distance which separates the individual from his fictitious goal, represented for
him by masculinity. On account of his sexual impulses he will
be prevented from facing whatever it is he fears as a test for
which he does not feel ready.

The impotent man and the frigid woman show hesitation,
timidity and tension at the idea that they may prove inadequate to the task. Their mind is centred on themselves and
their own reactions, seeking to blame their failure on un-
favourable external conditions, on the words or clumsy
actions of their partner. In this way the failure is not their
fault and their prestige is safe. The spirit of competition, here
also, harms the spirit of co-operation.

For Adler the solution which best answers present social
demands and the division of labour is monogamy. An individual shows his degree of co-operation and personal balance
in the way he approaches this problem. 'Love, with its fulfilment, marriage, is the most intimate devotion towards
a partner of the other sex, expressed in physical attraction,
in comradeship and in the decision to have children. It
can easily be shown that love and marriage are one side of
co-operation—not a co-operation for the welfare of two
persons only, but a co-operation also for the welfare of man-
kind.'[1]

The individual response in the sexual sphere is made in
accordance with the life-style, formed in the first years of life.
The sexual instinct is conditioned by the way the small child
sees and evaluates social life.

Neurosis

In the normal individual the search for superiority is centred
on the tasks which present themselves, and before which he
feels himself responsible. His social sense is developed and he
has maintained the courage necessary for an active response

[1] *What Life Should Mean to You*, Allen & Unwin, 1938, p. 263.

to the various problems. For Adler the neurotic is a person who has formed a mistaken opinion of himself and the world, and who has built up for himself a goal and a life-style which are both mistaken. In order to assert himself he has recourse to devices and tricks which he thinks will enable him to evade all personal responsibility.

The characteristic of Adlerian psychology is to consider neurosis from a purposive point of view, looking for the goal which the neurotic seeks to gain by it. The dynamism of the neurosis is the search for a goal of exaggerated superiority, in a way which will be of no use to society. It results in a set of symptoms corresponding to the individual's life-style, which provide an excuse for his behaviour and safeguard his personal prestige. The neurotic symptom indicates a deep internal insecurity, and flight into illness serves him as an excuse to dodge a decision and justify his inactivity or his failure. It is evidence of a frightened capitulation before the problems which have presented themselves.

The individual is not conscious of this protective mechanism and does not grasp the strict relationship which exists between his neurosis and his mode of life and he treats the neurosis as an illness which needs attention. He shows himself hesitant when action is called for, he depreciates others in order to show himself stronger than them, he makes accusations against his family and those around him, the feeling of guilt becomes a weapon in his hands, he creates obstacles and difficulties, he imposes limits upon his own action: in a word, he narrows his horizon in order not to experience defeat. The neurotic would like to... but cannot. The personality as a whole includes the neurotic symptom and is responsible for it. It may be the individual's personal goal which triggers off the neurosis, but it is the organ weakness which indicates the choice of symptom. It is not by chance that the illness takes the form of asthma or attacks of vomiting. The psychological troubles brought about by anxiety in face of a difficulty which he fears he is not ready to meet are related for each person to the organ which has been rendered susceptible by some hereditary weakness. Adler, speaking of 'organ jargon', that is to say of the functional response given by the organs under the pressure of external influences, has opened the way to psycho-somatic medicine, which is still in its infancy.

For Individual Psychology the way to treat a neurosis is to look for its mechanism; looking at it from the point of view of purpose enables the essential to be grasped. For example, in the case of a man who is running away from marriage it is the fact that he is making excuses that is the important thing—his work is too demanding, he has family responsibilities or bad health, he suffers from impotence, he is not earning enough. Bit by bit he must come to see that all these things correspond to what is imposed upon him by his life-style—to avoid marriage at all cost in order to hide his fear of certain responsibilities. The cure of the neurosis does not consist in the disappearance of the symptoms but in the complete modification of the person's attitude towards life. During the treatment the patient should develop a more satisfactory method of interpreting his own experiences than that which he has used hitherto and which has taken him so far from reality and from life. Therapy should be directed to securing a revision of his scale of values.

His initial error has resulted in an attitude of fear, and a consequent spirit of competition and combativeness, which takes him further and further away from other people. The task of the therapist, if it is possible to summarize in a few words something which develops as it goes along, is not limited to understanding the patient's mistakes and getting him to see them himself; this preliminary work, necessary as it is, is only the starting point of the real work. The most difficult thing is to act as a link between the patient and the society with which he has lost all contact.

'The task of the physician or psychologist is to give the patient the experience of contact with a fellow-man, and then to enable him to transfer this awakened social feeling to

other people.'[1] A patient's ability to recognize the mistakes
in his life-style depends not merely upon logical and emotional conviction, but also upon the growth of new courage
to enable him to accept them. The most difficult part consists
in developing his social sense, that is, his co-operation. In
order to recover the patient has to recognize that he wants to
recover, and that he is himself responsible for the success or
failure of his treatment. The idea of shouldering this responsibility is the first stage of the actual recovery. Moreover,
Adlerian psychology aims at enabling the individual to progress and educate himself in the future, so as to be able to
know how to respond to the difficulties which will present
themselves later on.

Neurosis is not the only type of adaptive failure. It is the
passive attitude, in which the person seeks to dominate by
exploiting his weakness. Without openly saying 'no' to the
demands of society the neurotic just produces a false reason
for his failure to co-operate. He would very much like to but
feels incapable. On the other hand those who have remained
fully active, but have developed their activity in the wrong
direction, are liable to be drawn towards delinquency, alco-
holism, etc. They say 'no' to society quite squarely. The
difficulty in the way of their readjustment consists in the fact
that all punishment increases the feeling of hostility which
they have for the whole world and gentle treatment only
makes them despise those who treat them so, since they ad-
mire violence. For them also the goal is to change their life-
style, to direct them towards social co-operation.

Dreams and Early Memories

From the Adlerian point of view the most fruitful material
for a study of a personality consists of the earliest childhood
memories, dreams, the position of the child in the family
constellation, any special childhood difficulty, external fac-

[1] Adler, *Problems of Neurosis*, Routledge and Kegan Paul, 1929, p. 20.

tors which may have occasioned the difficulty, such as illness, the birth of a brother or sister, starting school, changing school, a death in the family, etc. A person's childhood memories have already undergone a sorting, an elimination, a selection, to make them accord with the affective tone, the interests—in a word, the life-style of the subject. It does not matter much whether these memories are true and refer to a real situation, or whether they are a pure fiction of the imagination: the important thing is that the subject considers them to be his own. These memories constitute for him his life history, and serve as a scheme of reference in such a way as to encourage or depress him, to direct him towards a goal and to give him the means of comparing past and future experience.

Adlerian psychology interprets dreams with reference to the future. The contents of a dream may be forgotten, but something remains, a sort of general impression left by the dream. The purpose of the dream was to stir up these feelings. Dreams, like memories, serve to reinforce the life-style, encouraging those who are ready for action and, on the contrary, checking those who, by recalling past memories of failure, are looking for reasons to continue not believing in themselves.

Adlerian Psychology is in the first place a therapy, but it also seeks to be a prophylactic, trying by education to prevent the child making certain basic errors. In Vienna it is among parents and educationalists that the influence of Individual Psychology has shown itself particularly effective. Modern educational method has been permeated by it on account of the simplicity of its teaching, and its universal applicability. Individual Psychology guards itself against presenting a set of hard and fast rules for education but offers parents and teachers not only the means of understanding their children's character and reactions, such as inferiority feeling and compensation for it, position in the family, the importance of external change, etc., but also advice as to the attitude to adopt towards them. To educate, Adler says, is to encourage.

Adler has always had a keen interest in instructing teachers, because they are in a more objective position than the parents in relation to the children. The school, moreover, as the child's first experience of society in miniature, should have the double object of instructing and of educating children in the art of living with companions. 'We no longer wish to train children only to make money or take a position in the industrial system. We want fellow-men. We want equal, independent and responsible collaboration in the common work of culture.'[1]

Before concluding it may be of interest to consider Adler's position with regard to those currents of thought around him with which his contemporaries sometimes believed him to have something in common.

Although he was strongly influenced by Nietzsche and used the term 'will to power', it would be a mistake to think that he uses it in the case of the normal person. It only becomes an Adlerian term when it is applied to the neurotic attitude. From other points of view there are certain similarities of approach, such as philosophic relativism, an idea taken up by Vaihinger and used by Adler in this more developed form; also the theory of existential choice, based on courage and responsibility. In any case Adler's general attitude, based on the social principle, is opposed to Nietzsche's aristocratic individualism which despises all gregariousness. For Adler the search for power derives from an over-compensation for insecurity, resulting from a feeling not of power but of weakness.

Adler has always tried not to allow himself to be engulfed by certain groups who have thought they recognized an affinity with themselves in one point or another of his psychology. He tried to preserve the scientific character of Individual Psychology, keeping it clear of politics and religion. Certain Marxists tried to show that Adler's teaching

[1] Adler, *What Life Should Mean to You*, Allen & Unwin, 1952, p. 157.

had the same social orientation as theirs but the divergence between the goals of the two doctrines soon led to Individual Psychology being regarded as a manifestation of bourgeois conservatism. In fact Adler calls a person's attention to the need for changing his own character rather than social conditions. He was, however, far from being uninterested in social conditions: with his generous and all-embracing nature he never forgets to emphasize that in speaking of co-operation he is not only thinking of co-operation in the established social order, but of human co-operation in general *sub specie aeternitatis.*

With regard to religion Adler made his position clear for the benefit of those who thought that towards the end of his life he was turning towards religion, and of those Christians who thought they could recognize in his idea of social interest another way of describing the love of our neighbour. 'While the materialistic view lacks the goal, which after all is the essence of life, the religious view, far ahead in this respect, on the other hand lacks the causal foundation.'[1] He thought that Individual Psychology should remain within the confines imposed by its scientific character, while sympathizing with the movements whose goals are orientated in the same direction as its own.

If it is possible to link Adler's work with the currents of thought which attracted him, it seems that Christianity, democracy and Socratic rationalism were the three tendencies which attracted him most. The three have a similar standpoint in the moral controversy concerning the rights of the individual and social obligation.

Individual Psychology, which Adler wished to express in clear terms and illustrate by everyday examples in order to make it available to as many people as possible, is a rich and limitless mine of teaching. This brief summary has not been

---

[1] *Religion und Individualpsychologie,* Leipzig, 1933, p. 60; H. & R. Ansbacher, *op. cit.,* p. 461. Cf. L. Way, *Alfred Adler: An Introduction to His Psychology,* Penguin Books, 1956, p. 51.

able to do justice to all the human values which it contains—
respect for the individual, the art of human relationship,
optimism giving rise to confidence in oneself and in life,
freedom of choice.

Adlerian psychology has opened up many fields of study
and so it will continue in existence, because it is a beginning
and not an end.

THE PSYCHOTHERAPY OF
C. G. JUNG[1]

Dr Roland Cahen

From the time he met Freud, dreams and the psychology of dreams became Jung's principal instrument of research. We must pause a moment here, because in Jung's psychotherapy, in contrast to what has happened in the Freudian school, dreams have never ceased to increase in importance.

I. The Psychology of Dreams

Jung considers it a mistake to try and explain dreams with the help of categories and a psychology borrowed from consciousness. Dreams reflect a kind of functioning which is independent of the conscious purposes of the ego, and independent of its desires and intentions. This functioning appears as an apparently purposeless unfolding, like all development in the world of nature. It follows that it is in the psychology of dreams that theoretical presuppositions receive their most violent rebuttal and that they are least at home.

1. Freud was always inclined to regard dreams as being the manifestation of a mental life already near to psychological disorder, or as a kind of psychological activity which, if it grew much worse, would be well on the way to a pathological

[1] From an article in the *Encyclopédie Médico-Chirurgicale*, 37814 A 10 and 20. This part reproduction is by permission of Roland Cahen and the Encyclopédie.

state. In dreams he saw hysterical, obsessive or delusional
symptoms which were meaningless in themselves but indicated some more or less childish desire. Jung managed to
free himself completely from these presuppositions regarding
dreams.

He came to see in dreams a spontaneous, normal, creative
expression of the unconscious in imaginative and symbolic
terms.

As a result of this divergence of approach Freud was mainly
concerned with looking for the complexes and pathological
disorders which the dream might be concealing, without
paying much attention to the actual dream, which he rele-
gated to the order of means to end, whereas Jung, in contrast
to this, was concerned with the meaning of the dreams themselves.

2. Jung has criticized Freud's work on the psychology of
dreams but at the same time he has himself continued it. He
regards as valuable some of the data of the Freudian psychology of dreams, but objects to its narrowness and its one-
sided approach; in particular he finds the tendency to gather
all dreams into some sort of monism of desire, sexual or otherwise, quite unacceptable, however important the sphere of
sex or desire may be.

For Jung, in fact, the world of dreams is as rich, as varied
and as many-sided as the world of consciousness. Having at
its disposal all the factors relating to the ego and to consciousness, not only emotional factors such as pleasure and dis-
pleasure, but also ideas, perceptions and sensations, the world
of dreams presents a variety and richness which even surpasses
that of the conscious state; for the dream can appeal, in addition, to all the subliminal psychological material, memories,
perceptions and apperceptions, and repressions; it can appeal
to internal constructions and to all the potential psychic
material which has not yet reached the threshold of consciousness. In this limitless world, full of possibilities, dreams

have in Jung's eyes an importance which it would be impossible to overestimate: a dream for him is the situation present and structured in the unconscious at that particular moment, spontaneously representing itself and describing itself. Dreams therefore present a kind of report of what is going on internally at any given time.

Research has shown that a dream may be a simple reaction to a situation, with consciousness as the determining factor, or it may be composed of manifestations which are quite spontaneous and native to the unconscious, without any conscious stimulation, as it were. Between these two extreme possibilities may be found all the degrees from one to the other, and all possible combinations.

Jung is also unable to accept as a general principle the idea of a dream as a façade. Far from being 'only so and so', a dream is often exactly what it is, that is to say, a valuable expression of the interior life as it is structured at that moment, needing to be taken in its quasi-literal sense, and which, without calling for any theory of any kind, leads straight to the dreamer's secret garden.

3. In practice, when a patient brings him a dream the practitioner, according to Jung, should be able to put everything out of his mind except for one or two working hypotheses, which he should employ according to the nature of each individual case with tact, flexibility and moderation.

4. A knowledge of the life-history of the dreamer is an indispensable condition for beginning the work of dream interpretation. This life-history should be as complete, as precise and as detailed as possible, and should include the family history, type of education and subjects studied, intellectual and religious formation, profession, marriage, past and present environment, and any external catastrophes or interior struggles.

5. Since dreams are the exteriorization of the depths of the psyche, which has to express itself in the only language it has at its disposal, that is to say with imaginative material, archaic, primitive, personal or collective, they appear in general as mysterious messages, in the first place completely incomprehensible. To start with, Jung, like Freud, considers that free association will, in each case, provide the key to this language, which is not known to anyone, even the dreamer.

It is the individual's associations which will provide the alphabet, vocabulary and dictionary of his dream language, the origins of which are partly personal and partly occasioned by external incidents.

Jung handles this free association with great delicacy: what he tries to do is to prevent the dreamer losing himself in chains of associations which will go off at a tangent, whatever the context, and lead to those complexes which are active in him at the moment, but for which evidence is no longer required, and the existence of which no longer needs to be demonstrated—complexes which, there is good evidence to show, in normal or pathological form are found in everyone. Jung tries to concentrate the associated material around specific details of the dream, preventing by this circular movement any flight of ideas towards the infinite, and enabling light to be thrown on the details of the dream so that they can be seen in all their shades of meaning. However, this method of free association is only illuminating to the extent to which personal thematization is involved. Jung says that some dreams, or some elements in dreams, leave the dreamer without any association at all. This was one of the points on which he started diverging from Freud. Instead of getting dogmatic and obstinate, as Freud did, about the idea of resistance or of the censor—ideas which, of course, in some cases retain all their fundamental value—Jung conceived the idea that this aridity of ideas and associations on the part of the person being analysed pointed to the fact that there was

question here of a psychic element which had never yet been
in relation with his ego and his consciousness; this element
he regarded as arising spontaneously from the deeper layers
of the psyche to make what might be its first appearance in
the light of consciousness, whether the element in question
was one concerned with personal synthesis or whether, on
the contrary, it was an element which, although arising in
the subject, had not been acquired by him as an individual;
in this case it would be an unconscious element, existing
beyond the personal levels of the unconscious, and therefore
an element of the collective unconscious.

6. In cases where all the resources of association have been
perseveringly called up and exhausted but without success,
Jung considers that the practitioner is justified in himself
trying some association, in order to bring to his patient's
knowledge some elements drawn from historic or ethno-
graphic parallels, that is from the general human and psychological heritage, which might get things going again.
Thanks to this method of amplification, which should, of
course, be handled with the greatest possible care, Jung has
shown us how to get out of many an impasse. In practice the
use of this method makes it possible to present a subject with
one or more of those universal human problems which are
usually beyond the reach of consciousness and which the
subject did not even know was burdening him, even though
these problems may have been slowly fermenting in him for
years or even decades.

Free association, together with the life-history of the
dreamer, should in this way provide the personal alphabet
of his dreams in so far as material and data of the personal
unconscious are concerned; the analyst's amplification tries
to do the same for the data which arise from the layers of the
collective unconscious.

And so amplification appears to be at one and the same
time a practical method of unblocking an impasse and a

method *sui generis*, made necessary by the existence of problems linked with the collective unconscious.

7. The work of dream interpretation may be divided into
three stages:
(a) the dream takes place;
(b) the dreamer and the analyst proceed to collect the associations, and, if appropriate, any necessary amplification
is made;
(c) they may then, but not until then, set out on the adventure of interpreting.
   In practice it may be said that it is the second of these
three stages which needs the most careful handling; the first
is in fact a mental automatism; the dream is more or less
clear, more or less vague, remembered with more or less
sharpness and precision, but it is either there or it is not,
spontaneously and without the voluntary intervention of the
dreamer. In the third phase the practitioner is able to help
his patient and by co-operating with each other they can
travel together towards an interpretation which each of them,
by mutual agreement, can accept.
   In contrast with the first and third stages, the analyst and
analysand both depend in the second stage on the good will
of the subject's underlying associative mechanism for the
delivering up of the necessary associations, and also on the
ability of his consciousness to accept them; for the patient's
consciousness must be able or must become able to accept
these associations with something like the welcome of a
mother. For, we insist, without the dreamer's associations
his dreams remain a dead letter for all eternity, at least so
far as that which arises from the sphere of his personal unconscious is concerned.

8. To clarify things and make the analysis easier Jung suggests that the dream be considered as if it were a play in
four acts:

(a) The setting, characters, location, period, décor.
(b) The beginning of the action and the unfolding of the plot.
(c) The climax.
(d) The ending, solution, anticlimax, relaxing of tension, significance or conclusion.

Jung thinks that those dreams which end by the dreamer waking up with a start must be so important that the message or alarm signal has to be got through to consciousness, since they have succeeded in piercing all the psychological and physiological mechanisms which protect sleep.

9. A useful point to be remembered in practice is the idea of compensation. The subject matter of biology consists of self-regulating systems, and psychology, which rises out of it, is subject to the same norm. For Jung the psychic equilibrium of the individual is a balance between his conscious and his unconscious levels. For Jung, then, the relationship between a person's conscious position and the unconscious material constellated at any particular moment by the general situation, which of course includes the particular situation of his analysis, is more than a merely complementary one; the unconscious plays the part of a counterpoise, which comes in to compensate or widen the subjectivism, one-sidedness, desires, anxiety, defences and aspirations of consciousness.

This idea of compensation is quite easy to handle so long as we are concerned with the subject's personal problems. But the limitless complexity of the compensations which are possible in any given situation makes the idea of compensation very delicate to handle as soon as we have gone beyond the problems which are immediately practical or personal.

10. Freud took for his frame of reference the idea of instincts and impulses, and he accordingly subordinated his study of dreams to his general research into the causes of human behaviour; that is to say, his way of interpreting them is

essentially a reductive one, concerned with cause and effect.

Jung took full account of all that was valuable in this point of view, but he also showed its limitations and its inadequacy; he showed the necessity of adding to this causal-reductive point of view a point of view that would be prospective, synthetic and purposive:

(a) *prospective and anticipatory*, not in the sense of prophecy, but in the sense of looking for the energic process that might manifest itself during the dream;

(b) *synthetic:* mental life proceeds by way of an inevitable and necessary succession of mental syntheses. Every analysis, and every step in the analysis, is unconsciously and automatically followed by a re-synthesis. Dreams, with their related associations, provide the major elements for the analysis of a situation or of a person's life, but at the same time they also provide the elements which are necessary for synthesizing the analytic work, and what has taken place in the patient, and this they do with an unparalleled relevance and subtlety, just at the right moment, and in an almost organic manner, with unpredictable results.

(c) *purpose:* Jung has shown that purpose is inherent in all biological and psychological life and that efficient causes are often nothing but a means to an end. Whereas Freud asks what is the cause of a dream, and of what is it the symptom, Jung goes further and asks what is its goal, of what is it the sign, or even the symbol, thus making it possible for us to perceive the dynamic tendencies which are inherent in the self-regulating system of the psyche. So for Jung dreams may be at one and the same time an expression of the past, real, imagined or imaginary, a summing up of the present situation with its compromise between the way the person has to behave and his own psychic tendencies, and also the expression of a subliminal movement towards the future, still in process of being formed.

In order to avoid any misunderstanding let us repeat that analytic psychology, in every type of case, tries to combine the causal-reductive method with the prospective-synthetic: these are complementary aspects of one single thing.

11. *Subjective–objective:* another point which has to be considered, and which is indispensable to the interpretation of dreams, is the distinction between the subjective and objective points of view.

When a person dreams of a neighbour or of someone with whom he has important contacts, common sense invites us to find in the dream person the flesh and blood person of real life; the dream, then, might be reflecting an anxiety, an uneasy relationship, a problem of mutual adjustment, and would be a matter of projection; briefly, it might be expressing a concrete behaviour problem or some inter-personal tension, and this is an interpretation from the objective point of view.

But if the dream figure is that of someone with whom the dreamer has no social or business relationship, or is an imagined, imaginary or historic figure, this spontaneous common-sense point of view, which would incline to see a real person in the dream figure, is found to be completely useless. Jung has shown that in these cases it is necessary to think of the dream figure as being the embodiment of one side of the dreamer, of a part of himself, significantly reclothed and expressed by the figure which has been chosen: Gengis Khan, for example, would be the expression of the invading, conquering and destructive side of the dreamer, etc. This is an interpretation from the subjective point of view.

It is scarcely necessary to say that just as the reductive and purposive interpretations are complementary, so interpretations from the objective and subjective points of view are not in the least exclusive, but complement each other. In practice the point of view which is suitable to the external and internal situation of the dreamer has to be discovered by carefully feeling one's way, with continal reference to the dreamer's associations. Sometimes one point of view is used, sometimes the other, and sometimes the two are mixed together in varying proportions. Both points of view are fruitful; the objective interpretation will throw light on the subject's behaviour and the interpretation from the subjective point of view will help in the reflective and internal working out of his current problems. Interpretations from the two points of view remain interlaced right to the end; an alteration in behaviour can give rise to fresh reflections, of use to the subject in his development towards maturity and, on the other hand, the internal working out of problems can contribute powerfully towards an alteration in behaviour. This interplay between the subjective and objective ways of interpreting dreams is really nothing but an extension to the psychology of dreams of the interplay between introversion and extraversion, and the same major problems are encountered. The psychology of dreams must necessarily reflect the basic proposition that the external world is only one of the two sources from which come the impressions which bombard us, and that it serves at the same time as the framework for our internal elaborations.

In practice and as a general rule the objective point of view is dominant at the beginning of an analysis and gives way more and more to the subjective point of view and to internal elaboration. This general indication needs to be taken with a great deal of flexibility; the older the person being analysed the less suitable this indication may be expected to be. As G. Adler has shown with great clarity, there is a correspondence between the reductive and causal interpretation, which is essentially that of the objective point of view, and the prospective-synthetic interpretation, which is that of the subjective point of view.

12. Of cardinal importance is the idea of taking dreams in series. The strength and validity of dream analysis in psychotherapy does not come from interpreting a fragment of a dream, or a whole dream, or even several dreams; in the

course of such interpretation mistakes can always be made. It is the practice of taking dreams in series which gives such a sureness of touch to the work of dream interpretation. If a study is made of a succession of dreams, dreamed by one person over a fairly long period of time, certain themes are seen to be repeated, revealing a person's direction of development, under a slightly different form each time, and indicating the general orientation of his personality, that is to say the person's philosophy of life and his personal mythologems. If mistakes have been made during the course of the analysis, later dreams will provide a sort of commentary on previous interpretations, confirming those that were correct and disproving those that were at fault, thus making it possible *a posteriori* to rectify an unfounded doubt or an affirmation which had been advanced too categorically. This is due to the compensation mechanism we have just been talking about, which works through a subtle interplay between the conscious and the unconscious.

These dream series are very like a film with a number of different episodes and often seem quite like a serial story. To his no little surprise the therapist sees an internal consistency and a coherent ordering of the material where, until the time of Freud and Jung, nobody looked for anything but incoherence.

Just as in practice an interpretation never really exhausts a dream, but has to stop when sufficient seems to have been gained for practical use, in the same way one cannot exhaustively examine all the dreams in a series. This does not matter. Experience has shown that if anything of importance has been overlooked it will come up again later on: one dream which has been understood and well assimilated will enable the subject to make such progress that the fact that other dreams have been passed over for lack of time will not be of very great consequence.

13. Above all, and apart from all question of knowledge, the

analyst should be a good midwife, a good catalyst for the harvest of associations; a good interpretation of the subject's dreams creates a harmony between analyst and the person being analysed, both sides being able to agree with the interpretation put forward by both of them together. Neither for one nor for the other should there be any question of a sort of battle of wits. From the point of view of the treatment it would be troublesome and even positively harmful for the analyst to be in the right as against his patient, as this would put the latter in the position of a child and could give rise to a justifiable resistance. The need is to help the patient to reach something beyond a purely intellectual understanding. If analysis is for Jung 'the art of rich and creative silence', this is because it should, by means of a sharp moment of ideational metabolism, help the subject to feel within himself the subsiding of that psychological disturbance for which he is, as it were, the stage, and to participate emotionally in this subsiding, which is revealed in fragmentary fashion by his dreams, themselves only scraps cut off from a more continuous unconscious stream.

14. The practical use of the analysis of dreams lies in the fact that dreams contribute the point of view of the unconscious and that their interpretation opens this up and gradually aligns the patient with his own psychic depths. Everything takes place as if the analyst had slipped into the point of view of the subject's unconscious in order to help him to feel and discover, or even to tell the consciousness of his patient out loud and verbally that which his unconscious has been expressing by means of imagery. The point of view of consciousness should, of course, be taken equally into account throughout the work of analysis: it is only in this way that it is possible to bring together, to confront, and to harmonize these two major levels of the personality. There results from this a progressive succession of acts of awareness, each of which is accompanied by a rebound, a repercussion on the

unconscious. The act of awareness may be seen as the deto-
nator of a whole chain reaction which, travelling from link
to link, of which we only know a few, loses itself eventually,
as Leriche says, 'in the intimate silence of the tissues'.

In this way the analysis of dreams, through the interplay
between consciousness and the unconscious which it releases,
presides over a mobilization of psychic energy, over its liberation beyond the symptoms, and to a certain extent, over the
transfer of this psychic energy from the unconscious to the
conscious.

When a patient understands the meaning of a dream, a
meaning new to him, a fresh perspective has opened up for
him on such or such problem of his life, or on his life itself.
This widening of the conscious field is a process of major
importance for the mental life of every individual: a new
degree of consciousness is reached, which in its turn makes
fresh syntheses possible; it is the way of the integration of the
personality. In one sense it is life being given back to the
human person and this has been defined aptly by Lagache
as an integrating integration.

15. From a more general point of view, for a civilization to
accept the principle of the analysis of dreams is equivalent to
lifting the condemnation under which men's irrational
powers have suffered throughout the centuries; from this
moment the irrational is accepted by the rational as the
necessary transition between logic and life. Or, as C. A.
Meier says, the synthesis of conscious and unconscious psychic activity constitutes the very essence of creative work.

II. The Active Imagination Method

Both in theory and in practice the subject of dreams leads
directly to the important question of the imagination, both
passive and active.

1. *Imagination in general*. For Pascal and the traditional thinkers the imagination had long been the mistress of error and falsehood and it has been the privilege of analytic work, and of Jung's in particular, to re-establish the value of the imagination. Jung sees in imagination nothing less than the power which moves the world, and his psychotherapy may be usefully defined as the art of putting the imagination at the service of life, and life at the service of the realization of the imagination. There is nothing more stupid, he says, than to say, it is nothing but imagination. He considers imagination to be one of the major forms of mental activity; it is by means of the imagination that the ego perceives the underlying and underground part of psychic activity; it may be said with E. Minkowski that imagination, as opposed to a causal explanation, is the 'perception of the source'. As Bachelard has said, very rightly, imagination has many functions. Jung says that the imagination should be regarded as being in the service of the two basic attitudes of introversion and extroversion and the activity of the four psychic functions. The imagination is often the spokesman of the inferior function, in opposition to the dominant function, and should on this account attract the attention of the psychotherapist to the highest degree.

2. *The active imagination method*. Jung has worked out his active imagination method on the basis of this general description of the imagination. The method is as follows: the only effort the patient should make should be an effort of voluntary inattention, and he should let himself go, physically in a relaxed attitude, and mentally in a kind of drowsiness as if he were trying to go to sleep. In this attitude of physical and mental relaxation he should notice and express all the perceptions, ideas, feelings, and impressions which come into his mind or which present themselves spontaneously to his thought, and also all the images which are projected on to the black screen of his closed eyelids.

This method, which is one of active passivity, is of very great value

(a) in particular for use during those sessions when the patient cannot remember any dreams and has 'nothing to say' to the therapist;

(b) psychic material very like the hypnagogic imagery which precedes sleep or immediately precedes waking up is liberated by this method. This material has a psychological interest almost as great as that of the dream imagery itself; the layers from which it rises are not so deep as those of dream imagery and the interventions of consciousness are more obvious than in dreams, though they remain quite different from the usual content of consciousness; this imagery swarms with preconscious elements that are isolated by this method and can be followed in their more or less autonomous development. These elements can be of great importance for the patient's practical conduct, in so far as he becomes clearly aware of them.

This active imagination method really does nothing except bring into the foreground what Daudet has called the waking dream, and it does this by means of a voluntary withdrawal of consciousness. In the normal state this flow of dream imagery is diffuse and weak, underlying conscious psychic activity in a more or less permanent fashion, but kept in an imperceptible state by the blinding intensity of consciousness.

The heuristic criteria which we have described in connection with dreams may and should be applied to the products of the active imagination.

Jung's active imagination method, which has given rise to several derivative methods, is characterized by the fact that even here the analyst does not intervene and does not propose any subject for the reverie. It is strictly opposed to any attempt to impose any arbitrary pattern of working on the unconscious; the great virtue of the latter is its own proper activity, and the art of the practitioner is to facilitate the emergence, at the right moment, of those elements which need to come into being, and which should emerge in a quasi-organic context, as the result of the dreams, of the free association and of the active imagination. The analyst simply helps the patient to overcome his prejudices and any conscious holding back so that he may be able to welcome the material rising from the psychological non-ego.

Is there any danger of oneirism during the course of this inattentive but deliberate concentration on the interior imagery going on at the back of the mind, a concentration which allows one to seize unconscious processes on the wing, as it were, without having had any voluntary share in their formulation?

From our personal experience we can state that there is no such danger and that if it is properly carried out this method is perfectly harmless and constitutes a therapeutic weapon of major importance. The active imagination method takes its place within the general framework of analysis. Attention should be drawn here to the precautions which should attend the clinical indication of analysis as a whole; it should be emphasized that the active imagination method is by no means a parlour game, any more than any other part of analysis, and particularly because of the possibility of latent psychosis. It should not be had recourse to except in the setting of a stable affective relationship between patient and doctor. Moreover, not only is this deliberate attempt to descend into oneself quite free from the danger of inducing a state of oneirism, but it may even be regarded as one of the most efficacious cures for this state, since it provides an over-active unconscious with a safety valve which should lead to a more or less specific calming of psychogenic oneirism.

III. Drawing in Jungian Analysis

Following immediately on the interpretation of dreams and the active imagination, mention must be made of the use of drawing, which Jung introduced into analytic psychotherapy: after a dream, or an exercise of the active imagination which has left the dreamer with a strong visual impression, the practitioner asks him to fix the impression with whatever technical method is available and whether or not he is practised in its exercise.

All the different ways of looking at things which have already been described are relevant to these reproductions of deep psychic material, which are physical and pictorial expressions of it, as against the verbal expression to which reference has already been made.

Furthermore, the resulting drawing is a real diagram of the dreamer's unconscious psychology. What has up to then been an internal reality, on being drawn becomes an external reality, an object of contemplation and meditation and so capable of transforming energy. In the case of some patients, drawing has been found a more efficacious means of access to the fundamental symbols of the unconscious than language. This is understandable, because 'the value of such drawings lies precisely in the fact that these unconscious pictures possess a special symbolical power, for they come upon us with the full impact of a vision not yet watered down by any rationalistic process'.[1] An expression by means of imagery, since it is symbolic, possesses a 'magic force' like all symbols: one has only to think of the central role of pictures of divinities and saints in many religions.

We emphasize that there is no question of expecting works of art; generally speaking what the patients produce shows a very rudimentary technique. We are not concerned here with the aesthetic point of view. We are concerned with an alternative way of doing something, with helping a patient to allow himself to be influenced by his own active imagery, and enabling this active imagery to exercise a living action on the subject's consciousness.

In the same way embroidery, modelling, even dancing, etc.,

[1] G. Adler, *Studies in Analytical Psychology*, Routledge & Kegan Paul, 1948, p. 91.

can be used, according to the subject's particular gift and his particular need of expression.

These various ways of approach have given Jung a direct and detailed knowledge of human nature and have led him to assign a place of very great importance to a mode of expression which is not very common, but which none the less has been discovered to be one of the most important instruments of analytic psychotherapy—the symbolic mode of expression.

IV. Symbols and Archetypes

(a) Symbols

The psychological material liberated by dreams, the active imagination, drawings, etc., is often expressed in the form of symbols. This must not be taken as a sort of waywardness of nature, refusing to use the language people normally use. If some psychic elements are expressed in a symbolic form it is because nothing else is possible; symbols are the only vocabulary to which certain psychological levels have access.

Jung has shown that, in spite of the frequent confusion between the two, made worse by Freud, the word symbol must be understood as meaning something different from the word sign. The smoke going up into the sky may be a sign of the cottage hidden in the valley but it is not a symbol of it. 'The symbol always presupposes that the chosen expression is the best possible description, or formula, of a relatively unknown fact; a fact, however, which is none the less recognized or postulated as existing.'[1] A symbol is living so long as it remains the best possible expression of a thing and remains pregnant with hidden meaning. If this hidden meaning ever sees the light of day, in other words, if an expression is found to formulate more perfectly that which is sought, awaited, or glimpsed, from this moment the symbol which

[1] Jung, *Psychological Types*, Routledge & Kegan Paul, 1959, p. 601.

has been in use up till then is dead; it is now only of historic interest.

This idea of symbol is essential to an understanding of Jung's psychotherapy, Freud saw the multiplicity of dream images as more or less conventional signs, indicating sexuality as the smoke indicates the cottage, but Jung did not try to gather the variety of unconscious material into a theoretical monism, even into a monism that might be more or less diversified.

Having rejected the idea of referring to theoretical postulates which he had shown to be merely provisional and perhaps even false, Jung could not do otherwise than plunge into the study of comparative symbolism, seeking to find in the heritage of civilization, the history of religion, the psychology of primitive peoples, folklore, fairy tales, etc., what some imagery appearing perhaps in the dream of a modern European might have represented symbolically in the course of the development of humanity. It is this idea of symbols and what they stand for which, in part, led to the break between Jung and Freud in 1913 and gave his work the orientation which we know.

It is as a result of this research into comparative symbolism that Jung has been able to insert his method of amplification into psychotherapeutic practice, and that he has been able to show the consistency and universality of collective themes and to found so firmly his theory of archetypes.

Jung, then, accepted the full and complete meaning of true symbols; for him each symbol is the supreme expression of a psychic element inexpressible in any other fashion and often having a numinous character. His divergence from Freud was made even deeper by the fact that whereas Freud had in many cases seen the sign of a sexuality, the importance of which no one any longer thinks of doubting, Jung has shown that much sexual imagery requires to be understood in its turn as being symbolic of other psychic elements, and that to take it literally is to submit it to serious misunderstanding by making it too concrete: the penis, for example, is certainly a sexual organ, but throughout the whole of mythology it is also the symbol of creative energy.

Symbols have such pragmatic value because throughout the whole of human development they have been the expression and the repository of a whole major part of living, which could find no better expression than these symbols. It could be said that the advances of reason have constituted a continual encroachment on the world of symbols, reducing their number one by one. Today the life of consciousness may be able to dispense with symbolic expression to a very large extent, but one cannot say as much of the life of the unconscious. Today the psychotherapist meets personal, impersonal and trans-personal symbols all along the way, at every turning of the mental life of his patients, and it is necessary for him to be able to help these patients to extract the marrow from them, whether the subject retains them as living symbols, accepting their beneficial activity, or whether, with the help of parallels from history, he is able to grasp their import and integrate into his consciousness what was previously an irrational message, in which case they will be nothing but expired symbols. In the one case as in the other there is a major gain: symbols are not just an imaginative framework; they are able to release a considerable amount of potential psychic energy and Jung has shown that the role of symbols with regard to energy is that of real transformers, a sort of bridge which allows psychic energy to pass from one level to another; they should allow consciousness to realize what Jung has called the transcendent function of the psyche, that is to say the approach and conciliation in the human being of the rational and the irrational, the harmonizing and unification of contraries. Symbols are seen in this way as directing principles or pointers, as bridges between the present and the future and its goals; they are like 'diagrams of development', of the 'entelechy of the individual personality'.[1]

[1] G. Adler, *op. cit.*, p. 97.

From the practical point of view, if the subject can understand and accept these symbols it will enable him to assist in
the liberation and integration of the psychic energy now made
accessible to him, energy which hitherto has been diffuse,
blocked and out of reach, and has even been turned against
the subject himself, not only remaining useless, but actually
diminishing his overall activity. Furthermore, since symbolic
imagery always shares in the collective inheritance, it will
automatically help to take the subject out of his solitude and
isolation.

(b) *The archetypes*

Jung was led from the formulation of the consistency of certain symbolic patterns at all periods, in all civilizations and
in all parts of the world, to the idea of the archetypes. These,
as we have said, are a sort of complex, but an internal one;
they are forms or patterns which come, already structured,
to furnish and give life to the material of individual experience. 'The dispositions of the individual imply the existence
a priori of "organizing" factors, of internal ways of functioning.
These are the archetypes, the whole collection of which constitutes human nature. The chicken did not have to learn the
way to come out of the egg; it has it *a priori*.' The archetypes
may be compared to a skeleton, a potential framework for
the mental life. They are like a honeycomb in the cells of
which the materials of the individual life will be laid down.
The archetypes, as structures given *a priori*, provide a system
of functional dispositions, both for acting and for reacting.
In their capacity of being able to react to a future situation,
they are a kind of deep psychological reflex, an internal
necessity of the mind.

The archetypes find expression in the form of symbols, and,
as Bachelard has so rightly said, they are motor symbols. As
Fulchignoni says, the archetypes of the unconscious in their
dynamic flexibility may be contrasted with the stereotypes
of consciousness.

The question of the origin of the archetypes remains quite

obscure. In the last analysis we do not know where the archetypes come from any more than we know the origin of the
mind. All we can do is to describe them as the organs of the
mind, which can be no better defined than by using Bergson's
formula, 'eternally uncreated'; they may in fact be compared
to the plane structure of a crystal, which is contained in a
potential manner in the liquid from which the crystal will be
formed, and which leads to the particular formation of the
crystal, although in the liquid the formation does not actually
exist. The whole collection of archetypes in a particular individual constitutes what Kerenyi has called in a striking
phrase, the person's 'individual mythology'. Examples of
archetypes are the ideas of God, the devil, the soul, justice,
etc.

The practical importance of the archetypes comes from
the fact that they preside over: (a) our representational life,
the *imagines*, or symbol-bearers, those representations which
furnish our mind and live in us; the *imago*, for example, of
a parent is born of the encounter of archetypal data concerning parents with the individual dispositions met with by
the children; (b) our reactional life; (c) a great part of
psychogenic mental pathology, for 'archetypes were, and still
are, psychic forces that demand to be taken seriously, and
they have a strange way of making sure of their effect. Always
they were the bringers of protection and salvation, and their
violation has as its consequence the "perils of the soul" known
to us from the psychology of primitives. Moreover, they are
the infallible causes of neurotic and even psychotic disorders,
behaving exactly like neglected or maltreated physical organs
or organic functional systems.'[1]

Some archetypes have such practical importance for
psychotherapy that they call for an extensive consideration.
In this context we must be content with simply mentioning
them, because if we tried to describe them too briefly there

[1] C. G. Jung and C. Kerenyi, *Introduction to a Science of Mythology*,
Routledge and Kegan Paul, 1951, p. 105.

would be a risk of misunderstanding instead of clarity. I will just refer to the shadow, the anima and the animus, these two latter being the archetype of the soul in man and woman respectively, presiding over the life of relationship, and to the wise old man and the self.

The self in particular is the centre of the totality of the psychic being; it is the outcome of the process of the integration of the personality, a crystallization which, with complete spontaneity and by its own power, is sometimes occasioned by a course of analysis which has been well carried out and followed for a fairly long time. This psychic whole includes all a person's psychic life, conscious and unconscious, and all the basic psychological elements which we have only too briefly passed under review. If we were to emphasize one at the expense of the others we should be false to the spirit of Jung, who regards all the elements as fitting in harmoniously in the psychic whole of the human being, just as all the cells of the body are organically united in the biological structure. In the case of a neurotic there is a conflict between different elements in the personality. This idea of a psychic whole embracing the conscious and unconscious spheres, the macrocosm without and the microcosm within, is so wide and rich that it cannot be adequately conceptualized; any conceptualization must always remain asymptotic.

The self is the outcome of a process of development which Jung has described under the name of the process of individuation. This involves a symbolism, both individual and archetypal, concerned with finding a new centre and in the course of which appear unifying symbols or mandalas.

We touch here on a phenomenology which is completely empirical and also completely original: it is a result of the intra-psychic dialectic and it would take too long to describe it here. It is itself the result of a development conditioned, if I may say so, by a careful de-conditioning; this latter presupposes the working preliminaries which we have just been talking about. By means of the concept of the 'four levels

of action' it is possible to see the process of individuation in
the general perspective of analytic psychology.

V. The Four Levels of Action in Psychotherapy

Analytic activity looks from the outside like a very little
talking and a great deal of silence, but in fact it is so diverse,
so complex, so flexible that it would be vain to attempt to
reduce it all to a few uniform prescriptions. In his attempt to
find a framework wide enough to accommodate in their
totality and complexity the phenomena which appear and
have to be considered during the course of an analysis, Jung
always arranges his observations with reference to four levels
of efficacity.

The analysis acts:

1. On the level of confidence and confession, linking up in
this way with a truth which has served as the basis of many
initiation rites and many religious cults: this is the cathartic
action.

2. On the level of the transference, of the illumination and
of the analysis of the transference, which is necessary to dissolve the artificial bond which has spontaneously formed
between doctor and patient during the stage of confession.
Jung insists that the transference should be given only a
relative importance; the transference is a projective phenomenon which cannot be forced, any more than one can force
a belief. A subject does not project what he wants when he
wants.

For a psychological projection to take place there must be,
among other things, at least some slight degree of resemblance
between the unconscious representation projected and the
object on to which it is projected. Without this there cannot
arise that impression of identity which should set unrolling
the magic of his fantasy. And so the appearance of the transference will be for one person a sign that he is getting better,

for another a hindrance, or worse, while for a third the whole thing will be comparatively unimportant. This point of view has considerable practical value:

(a) because it makes it unnecessary systematically to terminate the treatment of those patients 'whom one has not been able to bring to a transference;'

(b) because, whatever one may wish, the transference is to some extent a convention of the treatment, useful in many cases, but which can on occasion take a harmful turn, invading the treatment and endangering its eventual success, despite the advantages which it may have presented at the beginning.

3. On the level of 'education and self-education'; once a patient has become aware of the psychic factors acting in him without his knowledge he should integrate them and from that moment should take account of them in his behaviour. Analysis is not art for art's sake, or knowledge for the sake of knowledge; analysis aims at a more perfect knowledge for the sake of more perfect action.

4. Finally, on the level of the transformation of the personality: the psychological action which takes place on the three levels already referred to will gradually bring this fourth level into existence. It is on this last level that the three earlier levels will melt together in a synthesis, the confession, the transference and the self-education serving as a springboard for a mysterious transformation of the whole being.

If these four levels of action are to be set going, it is necessary for the personality of the doctor to have had its blind spots removed, and to be as balanced and as mature as may be, so that no blind spot of his own may interfere with the development, the transformation, the re-centring of that personality with which, whether he likes it or not, he is going to find himself involved in an interchange, in a mutual inter-action: he should have undergone a teaching analysis, as Jung was the first to require.

A curious fact characterizes the history of modern psychotherapy: from each of these various levels there arises a rather surprising claim to be the only worthwhile sphere of action: and to each of them a school has sworn allegiance. This seems to arise from the fact that each of these levels of action enshrines a truth which, although in itself only partial, is none the less of fundamental importance; our world is so poor in solid truth that nobody wishes to lay his beliefs open to question, and this does not simplify the problem of scientific comparison.

VI. *The three Dimensions*

By making use, with discernment, of these four levels of action, lucidly abstracted from the experience in which they are enshrined, Jung re-unites the whole of the patient's life in these three dimensions: the past, the present and the future. This idea seems to follow quite naturally from his work.[1]

Here again Jung completes the work of his predecessors: of Freud, absorbed in the past, and of Adler, who is concerned with present adjustment. To these two important aspects of a person's life Jung adds a third, that of the future, which is being worked out in the individual as a result, among other things, of his innate creative activity, itself a result of his archetypal dispositions.

This third perspective is of the greatest importance; for, when what is necessary has been said of the past, is it not a serious evasion of the present and the future to remain at that point? And so Jung does not insist on Freud's retrospective point of view. He advises that it should be followed only if

[1] Psychotherapeutic treatment is composed of a succession of fruitful moments, or lived creative instants of tension. It may be said that the instant is the elementary unit of all psychotherapy, which is composed of a more or less lengthy succession of these instants. Each instant, itself, comprises a past which has given rise to it, a moment made present and a future in which it develops and dissolves. By breaking the single instant into the three dimensions of which it is composed we arrive in this way at a major working perspective.

the material requires. The necessity of re-living the past, of remembering, of putting into movement again all that which has been laid down badly or neurotically is beyond question. But one must not fall victim to the mistake of taking a temporal priority for a priority of value. Again, as far as possible, Jung gathers together all a person's past, as lived, believed, or imagined, and not for his mournful contemplation, but to allow him to understand how he is constituted at the present moment and to help him move forward into the possibilities of his own development.

So far as the present is concerned, with its current problems, Adler's psychology of intention retains all its value, at least for those who are in the first half of their life, but for those who have satisfactorily adapted themselves to all the exigencies of society it is completely sterile. In the case of these people a current balance sheet of their psychic functions, their energies and their psychological tensions must be drawn up; it is necessary to show them at length the significance of functional balance and one-sidedness—the problems of an introvert are not those of an extravert. An analytic psychotherapy which did not bring the doctor to see the necessity of helping a subject who is too introverted to become more extravert, and a subject who is too extraverted to become more introvert, according to the requirements of their internal compensatory movements which they have ignored for too long, would be unthinkable. In the same way a patient whose dominant function is thinking, for example, will present a completely different problem from that of a subject who is characterized by some other function. Jung, in demonstrating the harmfulness of a unilateral development of one function at the expense of the others, which then lie hidden and become trouble-makers in the unconscious, has shown the necessity of attending to the development of the lower function or functions; these function will assist in the emergence of the most unexpected material from the underlying subconscious. A function may be compared with a muscle: it cannot develop except by being used and by working; bringing each function into action raises particular difficulties and that is why psychotherapy is so painful at this stage for patient and practitioner alike. The practitioner ought to bring each one to ask himself exactly what, on account of his own one-sidedness, is particularly difficult for him, while being perhaps so easy for his neighbour; this requirement, which seems rather paradoxical, is necessary for the sake of his own complementarity and of a better harmony is his being: it is the orthopaedics of underdeveloped functions.

From then onwards the future takes on a new importance, and assumes a shape of which no hint was given by the past neurosis; a line of development, often opposed to the dominant function or the customary habit of consciousness, tentatively appears, and then becomes more precise, like a fugue, and asserts itself, expressing the contrapuntal potentialities of the person's development, with regard to both the personal and the collective, allowing the formative and normative value of the archetypes to see the light of day.

It is in this spontaneous and innate development, beyond all the limitations of our personalities and beyond all the mediocrities of our petty reasoning powers, that Jung sees the surest guarantee of the validity of psychotherapeutic activity. This is what he has been attempting to follow and describe for forty years of his existence, pointing out its crucial turning points and its laws and discovering important constant factors and a consistent correlation with the spontaneous development of the past as historically recorded. It is because of this correlation that Jung knows that all he has done is to rediscover, in the perspective of the natural sciences, natural processes which are not due to mere chance or to groping desire, whether instinctively sexual or irresistibly directed to power. Faced with a patient in this stage of development, Jungian analysis only seeks to act as a catalyst and to speed up the gradual growing and curative processes of nature: it is the way of individuation, that is to say the way which will create a real individual, steady on his psychological foundations, both personal and collective, well inserted into reality, to which he pays his due, well balanced in a flexible stance between the necessities of introversion and extraversion, between his past and his future, between his various functions and between his conscious and unconscious levels.

Is there any need to emphasize the advantage of looking at things from the triple point of view of past, present and future? A psychotherapy with an essentially reductive tendency must necessarily end in a kind of resignation which may sometimes be tinged with the shadow of despair, but a psychotherapy which is turned also towards the future, and accepts symbolic values as irresistible elements of future syntheses, is ever generating fresh values, and leaves the human soul all its potentiality for spontaneity and freedom.

TOWARDS A SYMBOLIC
KNOWLEDGE OF THE HUMAN
PERSON

Professor Igor A. Caruso

Among the various streams of thought which stem from Freud, many of them sharply contrasted, and sometimes even contradictory, there must be included the Vienna school of psychoanalysis which regards itself as open and personalist. The very compact paper which Professor Igor A. Caruso, Director of the Vienna Circle for Depth Psychology, has been kind enough to contribute, sets out the essential teaching of this school and takes its place naturally in the section devoted to Freud's successors.

   It will be seen that this doctrine, which has as its aim to renew the spiritual by psychoanalysis and psychoanalysis by the spiritual, is centred round a difficult but suggestive theory of symbolism.

It would be interesting to follow the development of ideas which, in the Latin and German west, among Roman Catholics and Protestants alike, has led to an individualist, positivist, rationalist and nominalist conception of man and of the world. Psychology is to some extent the test of this development of thought. Man as subject of knowledge obviously influences the picture that he forms of himself as object of knowledge. Conversely the picture he forms of himself also influences his attitude and behaviour. It would therefore be very foolish to imagine that psychology, above all depth psychology, could exist, without any connection with philosophy, as a pure natural science; in any case even 'pure' natural sciences cannot exist without some general idea of 'nature', that is to say in complete isolation from philosophy.

But it does seem that western thought has been very little inclined to unify its knowledge of the world. Such a unity is only possible if it is admitted that every branch of knowledge has an analogical relationship with all the other branches and that at every level of knowledge the symbol of a deeper and higher knowledge may be found. Thought is not rectilinear, like traditional logic or cause and effect determinism. It moves in a spiral, as may be seen in the Greek Fathers, from Clement of Alexandria and Origen to Gregory Palamas.

A living conception of the human person is only possible to a way of thinking that is analogical and cosmic. To a way of thinking that is rectilinear and nominalist the person inevitably becomes an abstract individual, or even vanishes into a collective concept.

We are beginning to rediscover the person in philosophy and in psychology. But the idea is often too nominalist and rationalist. For example psychology today often talks about mind, liberty, and even of the *homo religiosus*, but these are often quite abstract concepts, qualities of an ego always thought of as isolated and individualist. The person is not a mere meeting point between the individual and God—and an abstract God at that! The person is a real and living symbol of all the possible meetings between a concrete God and man in the concrete.

As neither God nor man are abstract concepts this meeting cannot be simply a meeting between two individuals. It implies a community: the revelation of a transcendent theandric community and the raising up of a human community to transcendence. The mystery of the Church could not be accomplished in the vacuum of juridic norms. The person is not an individual before God. The person is not the ego before society, and still less mind or idea in the abstract or the Jungian self. Here the Eastern Church can once more help us to a better understanding of what the person is. It is true that this understanding is not a rationalist understanding:

it is gnosis—but not gnosticism! It is not possible unless one believes in the mystery of a Trinity of Persons and in the Incarnation of the Son of God. The West is afraid of these analogies, because in the West theology itself is rationalist and nominalist. It is afraid that once these analogies are brought in the supernatural will be deduced from the natural. This is the reasoning of a rectilinear and causal way of thinking. It is quite obvious that the supernatural must not be allowed to appear as a consequence of the natural. For a unified thought, which moves in a spiral, everything in nature is a more or less obscure symbol of the highest level of thought. The new birth in grace, the Redemption and the life of glory are certainly incommensurate with man's natural powers, but these powers are a faint reflection, a poor symbol, of the new man's existence in grace and even of a personal God in his Incarnation.

The Fathers of the Church were not interested in psychology, because they spoke only in terms of a Christian anthropology, that is to say of the new man, sharing in grace and united to the Word Incarnate. But we are living in the twentieth century and we have a duty to share in its interests, however low they may be, in order to look for answers of a higher order.

All this is just by way of introduction to a personalist system of psychology and has nothing to do with apologetics. To tax our thought with being propagandist is to misunderstand it. We scarcely even mention religion during psychoanalytic treatment. All we do is to analyse religious problems in all tranquillity, thinking it better not to go too fast so long as instinctive complexes have not come to light.

This preamble is just a hypothesis of our own; for every psychologist, even if he is materialist and positivist, has a system of thought (*Weltanschauung*). It is always a matter of regret when this system of thought remains unconscious, because it then influences the psychologist's work without his realizing it. The psychoanalyst is in the same situation as his

neurotic patients, for they also are unaware of the real motives for their behaviour.

We think that Christian gnosis—not gnosticism!—is the
only *Weltanschauung* which is really 'catholic', that is to say
not simply rationalist, not simply irrational, but taking account of the unity of the person in a mode of knowledge which
is itself unified.

Neurosis or fixation is an existential heresy

In contrast with this neurosis is always an exaggeration of a
relative value. We call it an existential heresy.[1] This is not
looking at neurosis from an exclusively spiritual point of
view—which would also be a one-sided exaggeration of a
single perspective. We know from experience that Freud was
quite right to attribute the cause of neurosis to regression or
to a fixation at a temporary phase of development. A stage
of development is good in so far as it is a stage; if, instead of
being left behind it is made absolute, it takes on a negative
aspect. The fixation of the personality at an earlier phase,
which prevents it from attaining a balanced maturity, is then,
in the world of values, an existential heresy: it makes it
impossible for the personality to continue its progress, and
develop its potentialities of becoming a complete personality;
it prevents the personality becoming a transparent symbol of
God and the world.

We believe that it is insufficient to reduce symbols to their
instinctive basis, as in Freudian psychoanalysis; they should
also be transposed into the higher circles of the spiral. Every
psychoanalyst will have noticed that the same complexes,
the same symbols, keep returning during the course of the
treatment, but that they have a deeper or higher meaning
each time they return. The same action or the same imagery
may have an instinctive meaning and a spiritual meaning.

[1] May I refer the reader to my *Psychoanalyse und Synthese der Existenz*,
Herder, Vienna and Freiburg im Breisgau, 1952.

Erotic imagery may indicate a sexual complex, but also a religious attitude. The image of the father may indicate a childish phase of development, but also a definite and authentic attitude towards God. Freud introduced into psychoanalysis the fruitful concept of overdetermination, but with him the concept is still essentially biogenetic. But symbols should not be given an exclusively spiritual meaning either. In each case there is the risk of reinforcing the neurosis—the existential heresy: in the first case by strengthening the disintegrated forces of the id, in the second by strengthening the disintegrated forces of the superego.

Symbols are characteristic of personal existence in time

In order thouroughly to understand our personalist psychoanalysis it is not sufficient to know the preamble of religious gnosis—not gnosticism!—but also, more positively, our psychological hypotheses.

It would be a mistake to think that our Vienna Circle for Depth Psychology is primarily concerned with Christian gnosis, or with theology and philosophy! Our syllabus makes no mention of these subjects; on the contrary the student working with us studies biology, comparative psychology, psychoanalysis, clinical psychology, psychopathology, etc. But, as we have already said, every object of knowledge is a symbol, more or less opaque, of knowledge as a whole.

The idea of symbolism is central to any sort of knowledge and it is a remarkable fact that it completely disappeared in nineteenth century positivist and nominalist psychology. We should be grateful to Freud for having reintroduced it into psychology, although we should pass beyond his way of thinking, which remained, for all that, quite nominalist.

In order to understand the criteriological possibilities opened up by symbols, let us consider for a moment the object of psychoanalysis.

Psychoanalysis is concerned with a person's life-history, and this can only be understood by means of a multiplicity of symbols made concrete in the subject's behaviour—symptoms, dreams, activities, omissions, phases of development, artistic creations, etc. The personality expresses itself in time by means of symbols. Our research makes it possible for us to affirm that time, or, if it is preferred, history, is the primordial factor which makes symbolism both possible and necessary. In a state of life outside time symbols would be both superfluous and impossible; as St Paul says, so long as the image of this world endures, we cannot see face to face, but only through a glass in a dark manner. It is interesting to notice that the Apostle himself illustrated his thought by the phases of psychological development: he remarks that the child thinks and acts as a child, that a man thinks and acts as a man; and that in both cases our knowledge is only partial and imperfect.

This is exactly the line of thought followed by our personalist psychoanalysis, although we only apply it in one limited field, that of psychological development.

There has been much discussion about psychological structure and psychological functions. This discussion forms part of positivist and nominalist thought. It is forgotten that a structure is a pure abstraction if it does not actually express itself in functioning. Conversely, a function is a pure abstraction if it does not fulfil a role inherent in the structure of the organism.

It is important to note in this connection that most psychological and psychoanalytic ideas are nominalist: they have been, so to speak, hypostatized or personified; they turn into tyrannical myths because their purely symbolic value has been forgotten; the id, the superego, repression, agencies and layers of the mind, are all myths which, only too often, have been deprived of their symbolic value. Some people have tried to demythologize theology with the help of psychology. But it is psychology which should be demythologized first!

Symbols are imperfect knowledge

We may say, therefore, that a function, whether normal or maladjusted, retarded or precocious, is the symbol of a structure expressing itself in time. The structure is the genetic origin of the function—this is the reductive point of view, which is the only one known to traditional psychoanalysis—but it is at the same time the end or goal of that function. The concrete function observed in the life-history of the subject, that is to say, observed in time, is a more or less transparent, and therefore also more or less opaque, symbol of a structure. It is more or less transparent because it shows that the structure is concretely realizing itself in the function. It is more or less opaque because the structure, being subject to time, can never realize itself completely in the function, but only approximately. For all knowledge is imperfect, and is only a reflection of perfect knowledge; but it is knowledge, nevertheless, and the characteristic of such knowledge is to develop in time, to move towards that complete realization which will be possible once time has been left behind.

Being a realization, but an imperfect realization, a symbol has, so to speak, two faces: one open towards that knowledge which transcends it; the other mysterious and incomprehensible. A symbol is never a picture or a photograph, but is always a *sym-bolon*, a message, an encounter, a call. For example, a symbol in a dream is always a sign of the subject's past history but it is also a sign of his future, of his personal aspirations, of his potentiality for development, of his vocation in the world. Psychological analysis is always accompanied by a personal synthesis, which we have referred to previously as an existential synthesis in order to emphasize its character of historical transition.

But personalist psychoanalysis has been able to show that this symbolic character, which is at the same time both historic and transcendent, does not only belong to dream imagery, pathological symptoms and other strongly over-determined manifestations, but refers to all psychological activity, because all activity takes place in time and so has a history. The most elementary perception has a symbolic character and therefore points towards a world of transcendent knowledge.

Perception is a symbol of knowledge

Even the most elementary perception is never a simple photographic image of the external world. It is always the result of a meeting between a subject endowed with a certain organization and having a personal history, on the one hand, and a world of objects on the other. Modern animal psychology, as for example the work of A. Portmann, Tinbergen and K. Lorenz, has shown that an animal, by means of its internal organization, forms a unity of action with specific sectors of its environment, selected according to its needs. An animal is obviously very limited with regard to this unification, whereas the human person has almost unlimited possibilities. [1]

The human person also forms a unity with certain sectors of the external world. We cannot, for example, perceive infrared rays. And our range of perception will vary according to our personal history; the way a baby sees a woman is not the way in which a young man or an old woman will see her.

[1] It should be noted that the principle is not affected by the fact that at lower levels of life the individual is not an independent subject and does not have any subjective life, since it is nothing but a link in a chain, carrying out the instinctive reactions proper to its species. At this level the unity of action is formed by the species and the requisite environment. Throughout phylogenesis, and when we come to higher organisms, throughout ontogenesis as well, there may be perceived the law of an increasing degree of personalization. Jung's genius, imprisoned as it is within the framework of positivist thought, has interpreted this law in a completely mistaken fashion by turning it into nothing but an individuation. But for a Christian the highest flowering of personality is promised in the Communion of Saints and the Blessed Trinity is for him the inexpressible archetype of all personal life. There cannot be question here of any individuation but rather of a transcendent personalization, of which the pale reflection may be vaguely caught even in phylogenesis.

Selection of the external world is differentiated for the child according to the various stages of development that he passes through, as Sigmund and Anna Freud have shown.

The symbolic character of perception implies a dynamism which transcends mere representation. No perception would be possible were there not in the subject's organization and history an openness towards the future which makes possible this subject-object unity. In every perceiving subject there must therefore be a prefiguration of possible perception; what V. von Weizäcker has called prolepsis. Our master, A. Auersperg, has rightly insisted on the fact that in consequence of this there can be no question of any purely causal production of perception, but that the subjective and objective sides are in a specific relationship which he has called a 'meaningful coincidence'; the word 'coincidence' is taken, of course, in the strong sense, and not in the sense of 'by chance.' In any case the idea of mere chance is absurd outside nominalism; since every contact with the world has a symbolic character, fate also has a symbolic character, both with regard to the human person and with regard to divine Providence.

The superego is a symbol of conscience

Another example taken from psychoanalysis is the symbolic character of the Freudian superego. For Freud, conscience and the superego were identical; more precisely, conscience was nothing but anxiety resulting from a repressive superego. This is not surprising since Freud—like the moral theology of his time—only thought of conscience in legalistic terms and seemed to have no idea that a human being could be conscious of a law which ruled creation other than by its purely negative aspects, such as prohibitions, punishment, anxiety. The Freudian superego is of narcissistic origin: the libido starts off by loving the ego, and is then gradually transferred to an ego-ideal, that is to say an unreal representation of the ego, resulting from the requirements of authority. The ego-ideal, accepted as if it were real, accommodates itself to these requirements and fights all the instinctive impulses which threaten to refute the ideal representation obtained in this way. Narcissistic in its origin, the love of the ego-ideal gives rise to a repressive and aggressive agency to which Freud has given the very expressive name of the superego. This name is very expressive; there is no better way of indicating the egoistic, arbitrary and nominalist character of morality, whether atheist or would-be religious, when it does not arise from the love of a free person for another free person, and above all for a personal God.

However, it is obvious that this freely given and disinterested love cannot be reached at any or every stage of a man's development. It cannot be truly realized until knowledge is 'face to face' and no longer 'through a glass in a dark manner'—that is to say dependent on symbols.

Psychoanalysis has shown that Freud's theory of the superego is based on easily controllable observation of the transition from self-love to love of another. We have seen earlier on that each phase of development corresponds to definite sectors of the internal or external world, and psychological analysis has shown that Freud was not mistaken when he said that the love of the ego-ideal is narcissistic in its origin and aggressive in its manifestation.

But in doing this he reduced the whole problem to a single one of its aspects—that of its genesis. Like complexes, dream imagery, pathological symptoms, even elementary perception, the superego is on the one hand a symbol rising out of the subject's interior organization and life-history; on the other hand it is also an objective structure. The superego is a concrete conscience, developing with the individual: it is not conscience in the abstract, but an historically existing conscience, always imperfectly realized. In relation to conscience as such, a particular superego is, like every other symbol, at once opaque and transparent; opaque because it is the concrete realization, temporary and imperfect, of a function which is aiming at transcendence. It is at the same time transparent, because it is the sign of a progress towards the realization of this transcendent function.

It follows that the superego is at the same time an instrument and an obstacle. It is the instrument of fulfilment, for a structure which did not function in the subject's concrete historical life would not exist; it is therefore necessary to take account of its actual development, and a properly developed superego takes the personality on towards the idea of conscience. The superego is also an obstacle in the way of fulfilment, because the subject's concrete historical life, just because it is growth, does not permit the immediate and complete realization of the integrity of conscience.

Compared, then, with pure knowledge, the superego is a necessary evil or a relative good. It should not be broken too hastily. But on the other hand it should not be made absolute in the nominalist manner. Every teacher knows that the child is not very quick to acquire liberty of action, and that he needs in the first place to be given commands, and models to follow, and many prohibitions. At the beginning, according to J. Piaget, the child goes through a quite formalist phase of heteronomy. But a formalist morality is also the worst obstacle to personal maturity; it is, however, very widespread and betrays itself by an anxious perfectionism, by activism and voluntarism, by an apparent compatibility between formal sin and a selfish attitude to merit. This formalistic morality is a neurotic factor: on the one hand the person tends to identify himself with the ideal of perfection proposed to his ego; on the other he tends to suppress everything which is contrary to this ideal, and to become aggressive.

Ambivalence is characteristic of symbols

The preceding examples are sufficient to show that the human person cannot step straight into perfect knowledge and freedom, but has to develop painfully, following the direction which a mind sufficiently open sees will lead to knowledge and freedom. But these categories in their perfect state essentially transcend human conditions; here we see nothing but their reflection. And again, these reflections are not identical with themselves; they only become clearer to the degree that the personality painfully matures and detaches itself from narcissistic love in order to turn towards other people.

So, to talk about growth and development is necessarily to talk about failure, crisis, mistakes, faults. Psychology knows that progress is by trial and error. And as we have seen, symbols are attempts at knowledge; the same symbol may be, if one wishes, an instrument of truth or of falsehood; in a word, every symbol is ambivalent. Ambivalence is a condition inherent in everything that exists and not, as has been thought, peculiar to the schizophrenic or the neurotic. The normal man corrects his naive realism by a more flexible adjustment than the person who is mentally ill. But all fanaticism, all systematized delusions, all the extremes, consist in forgetting the ambivalence of symbols and in accepting them as the complete truth. Totalitarianism believes in the absolute truth of one symbol, and consequently in the absolute falsehood of some other symbol. The same process rules all totalitarian tendencies and all heresies, but also all psychopathic ravings: this is to make symbols absolute, which is the nominalist attitude towards them, hypostatizing them, or rather considering them as if they were things.

The remedy for this totalitarianism is neither relativism nor scepticism, but consists in being open to that transcendence which is revealed, and partly hidden, by symbols, because only this attitude makes possible the deepening of potential knowledge. Symbols are living realities which take us, step by step, towards knowledge; we must therefore be able to allow ourselves to be influenced by them without attributing to them an absolute value. As we have already seen, this attitude is the opposite of a utilitarian activism or selfish perfectionism. It presupposes the possibility of pure contemplation, so greatly despised by a utilitarian and symbol-less civilization. It presupposes also a certain humility. Curiously enough, even psychoanalysis, as we may notice every day, is only successful with humble minded people, who are able to accept themselves as they are—ignorant and feeble—and not as they would like to be. The value of a well conducted psychoanalysis is to teach the mentally ill the patience and humility necessary for them to arrive at a relative knowledge of themselves. Psychoanalysis is the opposite of activism and partakes of a contemplative attitude. Contemplation is cruelly lacking in the case of western man, even if he is religious, since he usually understands religion as morality and the search for perfection. Some writers wish to see in psychoanalysis a secular caricature of the sacrament of penance. It is rather a secularized contemplation; and every age has the contemplation it deserves. Despite all the mistakes of the traditional method of Freudian psychoanalysis with its determinism, its therapeutic success is incomparably greater than that of certain existential therapists, who are continually preaching freedom; for freedom is never given as a whole, but can only be obtained after a difficult liberation. Besides, freedom is situated at a level which is not accessible to any positivist science: freedom presupposes the rebirth of the person in love and grace. Origen, in an admirable passage, takes the saying of St Paul which we have already cited, and says that not only do we know 'through a glass in a dark manner' and not 'face to face', but that even the saints themselves are not free 'face to face' but are free 'through a glass in a dark manner', imperfectly.

This imperfection is inherent in our temporal and bodily life. But one cannot see better by despising the mirror or by breaking it! The Manichean hatred of matter, of instinct, of the 'flesh', forgets that matter is the condition of perfection and liberation, because the progressive liberation of the personality only arises out of the conflict between the bondage of the flesh and the liberty of the spirit. Consciousness and conscience both manifest themselves in our temporal existence through conflict and growth, and hence through ambivalence and tension. In practice, high talk about a freedom to be fully achieved by the resources of our own ego only serves to reinforce narcissism and the aggressive superego.

For aggressiveness is the price of being rid of ambivalence. Freud felt compelled to introduce the idea of a death instinct as a primary instinct, to which in the last analysis the libido would be subordinated. This pessimistic theory is absurd from the biological point of view, but in addition it is only made possible by a serious philosophical error. It betrays the impasse reached by a genius who, imprisoned in a formalist and nominalist system of logic, was incapable of conceiving that gnosis which alone could explain the analogies, parables and symbols of our ambivalent knowledge. Through trying to conceive of ambivalence outside a cosmic scheme of things which would aim at transcending relativity, Freud could not see death as the symbol of birth, but could only regard it as the goal of life. He sees only one side of the ambivalence— destruction, error, triumphant hatred of life and truth; for these last, relative and ambivalent, are only seen 'in a glass'. 'Unto the Jews indeed a stumblingblock, and unto the Gentiles foolishness.'

Even on the much lower level of psychoanalytic knowledge it is, nevertheless, obvious that the growth of the personality involves degradation, limitation and death to a certain degree. Each fresh stage of development implied the death of the preceding stage: fixation and neurosis would be unthinkable without this law. Every complex implies the degradation of an archetypal faculty; every symbol implies obscurity of knowledge; all functioning implies the possibility of abuse.

But it would be an existential absurdity and a neurotic

nihilism to remain here in this Manichean position. For every stage is also a progress, every complex is an attempt at a solution, every symbol is an approach to knowledge, every functioning a more or less successful realization of the archetypal structure.

Neurosis is a symbol of a religious drama

This enables us to understand that a neurosis is not only a biological process, but also a religious drama; and in consequence, that psychotherapy is not only psychological medicine, although it is necessarily that, but also—whether one wishes it or not, whether one admits it or not—a religious process.

Fixation and neurotic regression are snares along the path of the development of the personality, and so of knowledge and of personal love. We must be careful here not to fall into a Manichean attitude: evil and falsehood are not absolute values, even in neurosis; every fixation, every regression, is an attempt at a solution: the ego, as yet too little asserted, needs egoistic libido for the very possibility of developing. If a neurosis did not present any positive aspect, even and above all in what constitutes its essence, it would be useless and impossible to try to influence it. There is, then, a positive aspect in every neurotic symptom. Expert in pathology, and pessimistic in outlook as he was, Freud has emphasized the negative aspects of fixation and regression; he even invented the idea of a libido which was narcissistic in its very essence, because of his nominalist conception of it. The ambivalence, then, of all development enables us to say that the libido is simply the manifestation of a general law of growth; narcissistic to start with, its tendency is to turn into altruistic eros, and so to become a poor symbol of that which, on another level of the spiral, agape should be. This reflection of a higher level may be seen in the same way in all neurotic manifestations.

It is absurd, for example, for a religious minded person to see in the erotic language of the mystics a proof that religion is nothing but a superstructure of sexual desire. But it may offer proof that there are analogies at the different levels of being and, in so far as symbols are involved, they indicate an encounter between the organization and life-history of the subject on the one hand and a transcendent reality on the other. It would therefore be more precise to say, conversely, that even sexual desire is as much a symbol of the person's development as, on a different level, of his vocation.

This law also applies to neurotic symbols: they are symbols of a disturbed growth, but also of a call to something higher. It is necessary in psychotherapy to see the positive aspect of every symptom and neurotic mechanism.

Neurosis is caused by a fixation which makes absolute a value which should be relative and temporary. It is an existential heresy; but a heresy is always the sign of a tendency towards absolutism. The neurotic infantilism which results from fixation is certainly a faulty development, a flight from reality and a blocking up of life; but it is also an unsuccessful attempt to make real this world of religious knowledge which childhood is; it is a caricature of childhood, but also a poor symbol of that vocation which consists in becoming 'like little children.'

Neurotic fear means that a person is trying to keep to a stage in which he is seeking happiness; from this egoism and neurotic weakness both arise. But this happiness, sought in attachment to the narcissistic stage, is an imperfect image of that beatitude which is promised us once our ego no longer forms an obstacle to a complete personal union. Narcissism and total union are like the top and bottom rungs of a ladder which the neurotic dare not climb.

Imprisoned in a stage which is strongly narcissistic, the neurotic clings to a rigid superego, and we have already seen that the superego has a narcissistic origin. He represses everything which goes against the ideal, and false, picture of his ego; he is neither modest nor humble; that is what we have called the complex of angelism, for the neurotic refuses to accept himself as he really is, with his all too human aspects. This formalist and blind morality is also a caricature; but like all caricatures, it is modelled on something, here perfection itself: 'Be you therefore perfect, as also your heavenly Father is perfect'. The desire for perfection, united here to love of self, leads to a terrible impatience, and to terrible illusions.

This neurotic perfectionism has its reverse side: resulting as it does from repression, it projects the anxiety resulting from the repressed instincts on to a 'shadow', which the subject persecutes with his Manichean aggressiveness: this is what we call the scapegoat complex. The aggressive superego wishes to destroy the scapegoat—hence the terrible neurotic aggressiveness. But the scapegoat, which in any case is to some extent the neurotic punishing himself, in an image of the Saviour. Only he who is willing to take upon himself all sin and all suffering can deliver the person from his vicious circle. The archetype of the Saviour is very much alive in every neurotic soul and it is a positivist fallacy to try to explain the 'myth' of a personal Saviour by neurotic desire, instead of seeing that this desire also is symbolic.

Fixation and thirst for the absolute; infantilism and thirsting to be a child; selfish seeking for happiness and thirst for beatitude; perfectionism (angelism) and thirst for true perfection; aggressiveness (scapegoat complex) and thirst for a Redeemer: everywhere in neurosis we see the paradox of ambivalence. And we could continue indefinitely, because all human conflicts are to be found in neurosis. The Oedipus complex is not without analogy with the need to unite oneself to a 'catholicity' which is the 'bride of Christ'; the rituals of a compulsion neurosis (*Zwangsneurose*) have a magical character, and are thus a shadow of the sacred, and a caricature of the liturgy; the extreme need of love met with in hysteria can never be truly satisfied except by the personal and infinite Love which can take the human person out of himself. The paradox of ambivalence is the only true paradox, because it is inherent in symbolism, that is to say in the very mode of our knowledge. For the symbol is the point at which our immanence meets that which transcends us.

A personalist psychoanalysis should be able to understand this paradox; it should be able to look for the meaning of symbols: above all the meaning of the symbol of a religious drama, such as neurosis presents us with in a lower circle of the spiral.

It is hardly necessary to add that all this is quite opposed to a utilitarian position, which simply recognizes religion as very useful from the point of view of mental hygiene. The fact that 'religious' minds can arrive at such a pragmatic attitude only shows how far they cruelly lack a living relationship with mystery. Psychoanalytic practice has sufficiently demonstrated that there is nothing less hygienic than pragmatic religion. Deprived of all relationship with mystery, it can do nothing but reinforce the neurotic mechanism which turns relative values into absolutes.

Final remarks

These examples, taken from the scientific practice of psychoanalysis, have no meaning for anyone who does not know that religion is a more perfect mode of knowledge than any other. This essay therefore presupposes the preliminary datum of the faith and cannot commit anyone except the author. These notes would consequently seem quite absurd to anyone who thinks that religion is a mere phenomenon, separated, moreover, by watertight doors from all that we may learn 'scientifically' about man and the world. Among those who think in this way, there are positivist minds and 'religious' minds. In each case the conception of knowledge and of the human person is terribly superficial, or rather superstitious, the superstition of phenomenalism.

Several times in these notes I have used the Greek word *gnosis*, and someone may wish to take me up over it. This word, dear to St Paul, does not mean gnosticism. *Gnosis* obviously uses human reason, but to deepen Revelation as known in time, as it is accepted and interpreted by the tradition of the Church: it is the way of thought of a believer. Gnosticism is a system which in practice puts itself above faith, and therefore above Revelation.

To adopt the way of thought of a believer, a knowledge which collaborates with faith, is to understand that it is possible to be a serious student of the positive sciences and yet at the same time accept wider and more universal modes of knowledge. There is no value in this, not even a relative value, unless great care is taken to accept provisionally only those hypotheses which fit into the framework of a unified vision of the world: symbols are not monads, but the reflection of a reality which can only be one.

Starting from the human person, as from this glass through which we see in a dark manner, we may certainly come, slowly and painfully, to a glimpse of a transcendent personal order; but only faith can give access to this transcendent order, never reason or moral perfection. Because access to this order is neither a matter of reason not of morals: it can only come about through a new birth.

And this is another reason for rejecting gnosticism. Whether it arises from ancient heresies, from Plotinus, from theosophy, or from Jung's psychologism, gnosticism degrades the transcendent order to a mythological system. All these systems, therefore, necessarily lack faith in a transcendent mystery.

This mystery cannot be 'explained' by psychology. The God of the philosophers is not the eternal Father; the Logos of Plotinus is not the Word Incarnate; the spirit talked about so much by a certain fashionable psychology is not the Comforter who proceeds from the Father and is sent by the Son to his Church.

Meanwhile nature carries within itself the last reflections of this mystery and groans in the expectation of its final end, which will also be a return to its origin.

BEYOND PSYCHOANALYSIS

PSYCHOANALYSIS AND PHENOMENOLOGY

A. Vergote

'One could almost say that water is mad, on account of this hysterical need, which possesses it like an obsession, to obey nothing but its own gravity.'
Francis Ponge, *Le Parti pris des choses*

In this natural inevitability we see the familiar reflection of a human face. Since Freud it is no longer possible to define man simply in terms of his power of speech, or of those metaphysical aspirations which carry him, even without his realizing it, towards the search for truth. He is also this creature that we see threatened with psychic disequilibrium and mental illness, not only by an accident of his physiological constitution, but by the force of gravity which is to be found at the very heart of his intellectual development.

The wisdom of the ages knows that genius is akin to madness. Freud has shown us that this spark of genius sleeps in every man, bringing him close to neurosis and to madness. Like the gods, men walk along fragile bridges, suspended above a chasm. '*Amor meus, pondus meum,*' said St Augustine. It is the selfsame love which carries a man upward towards his destiny or insidiously draws him towards the chasm of madness.

Making fun of his naive audience, Molière brought the degradation of ethical purity on to the stage in the madness of the *Misanthrope*. Hegel denounced that secret passion, lurking behind the virtuousness of the 'beautiful soul', which leads to the madness of fanatical and subversive intolerance. Kierkegaard for his part pronounced the psychiatrist, thinking himself safe from all threat of madness, as more stupid than his patients.[1] Freud takes his place in this line of observers of men, pointing out that the peculiar characteristic of man is to be discovered in a detailed consideration of apparently dehumanized human acts. And it is here that he links up with another current of thought, that of phenomenology.

Phenomenology now has as many variations as psychoanalysis, but certain considerations are common to all the schools. These considerations may be regarded as fanning out from the concern, common to all those who claim to be descended from the founder, to purify philosophic thought of all traces both of naturalism and idealism. Even if some of Husserl's own developments seem to tend towards idealism,[2] phenomenalism nevertheless retains its character as a permanent attempt to restore to philosophy its original task, and to save it from the two forms of madness towards which it is inclined to slide, apathy and fanaticism. Phenomenology wishes to re-establish man in his true being, a manifestation of meaning against a background of the meaningless, speech emerging from nature and remaining attached to nature though transfiguring it, intention freeing itself from the hold of the past from which it arises.

Neither psychoanalysis nor phenomenology sprang up out of nothing. Freud is very conscious, more sometimes than are his admirers or critics, of continuing and making articulate the intuitions of literary geniuses such as Shakespeare, Goethe and Dostoevsky.[3] Phenomenology, thanks to its founder and his unphilosophical cultural background, has rediscovered the original inspiration of philosophy—the study of human meaning. The profound revolution brought about by Husserl

[1] *The Concept of Dread*, Princeton, 1944.

[2] This interpretation is mistaken because it places Husserl in a context which is not his. See E. Fink, *Problèmes actuels de la phénoménologie*, 1952, pp. 68–71.

[3] For the decisive influence, for example, of Goethe, see Freud, 'A Childhood Recollection from 'Dichtung und Wahrheit'', *Collected Papers*, IV, p. 357.

consists in the fact that he systematically describes in a new light some essential mental operations that philosophy before him had been using in the semi-consciousness of its creative spontaneity.

This attempt at a fresh clarification shows a surprising kinship with the original purpose of Freudian psychoanalysis. Freud also moved on the fringe of the official schools of psychology, and he reconquered the field proper to psychology as Aristotle conceived it—the study of the human mind in so far as it expresses itself in the parallel disciplines of logic and ethics, at the very source of theoretical and practical activity.

Freud and Husserl are grouped together in the history of European thought by reason of the publication dates of their first important work, if by nothing else. The *Logische Untersuchungen* appeared in 1899 and the *Traumdeutung* (*Interpretation of Dreams*) in 1900. Both men were pupils of the philosopher Brentano, and it is more than probable that Freud as well as Husserl was influenced by him.[1] As they both lived in an atmosphere of psychologism and neo-Kantianism, it must have been at the lectures of this Aristotelian-Thomist philosopher that they discovered those essential principles of western philosophy which have since proved themselves so very fertile. If the misunderstanding between Freud and philosophy has become proverbial, he has left us, nevertheless, a whole philosophy in practice. Lenin's judgement on Marx may be applied equally to Freud. No more than Marx did Freud construct a system of logic. But like Marx he has left us one in the concrete analysis of the phenomenon of man. The central and revealing human fact of which the analysis by Marx constitutes a logic in action was the idea of capital. For Freud it was the development of the libido, understood in the all-embracing sense of the eros of the philosophers.[2]

---

[1] Cf. E. Jones, *Sigmund Freud, Life and Work*, Vol. I, pp. 61–2, London, 1953.
[2] *Group Psychology and the Analysis of the Ego*, Standard Ed., Vol. XVIII, p. 91.

The relationship between phenomenology and psycho-analysis is so close that it is often thought, on one side or the other, that effective contact between these two lines of thought is of absolute necessity for the development of the two sciences of man. Sartre has even thought good to substitute the ex-pression existential psychoanalysis for that of existential phenomenology,[1] and a well known school of psychoanalytic research wishes to be known by the name of existential ana-lysis. The discussion has been opened. We may well consider both its usefulness and its ambiguity.

I. Freud's discovery of the psychic as bearer of meaning

The book which inaugurated the analytic era carried the title, *The Interpretation of Dreams*, which the French trans-lation rendered in quite contrary fashion as *Science des rêves*. Freud made a complete summary of the various sciences of dreams in the first chapter, and his interpretation of dreams was set out in opposition to any such science. Jaspers was not saying anything new when he applied to psychiatry the dis-tinction between description and understanding (*erklären* and *verstehen*),[2] which was in general use in Germany in the nineteenth century for distinguishing the mode of intelligi-bility proper to the natural sciences and social sciences respectively.

When Charcot, in the course of his hypnotic sessions, grew impatient because of his patients' resistance, Freud took their part, and was indignant at the violence done to their psycho-logy.[3] He thought that the patients must have good reason for resisting. He suspected that their illness was due to motives that were real enough, although they could not admit them to themselves. How then could violence be right as against a motive that the patient was clinging to with all his being? In this first intuition was contained in germ the whole of

---

[1] *Being and Nothingness*, p. 557.
[2] *Allgemeine Psychopathologie*, p. 290.
[3] *Group Psychology and the Analysis of the Ego, op. cit.*, p. 89.

psychoanalysis. Morbid symptoms could not be got rid of by external action, by a direct causality practised by one being on another. Psychological illness is only in the power of the sick person himself, because it *is* the meaning that he gives to his life. And what Freud will later discover by the slow working out of the analytic technique is already in action in this astonishingly clear intuition—that resistance to treatment has a profoundly human significance. It is not a phenomenon incidental to the illness. Nor is it a deception. It is the manifestation of the second force involved in the illness.

It was a certain Anna O., suffering from hysteria, who revealed to Freud that all neurotic symptoms have a meaning —inability to drink and anorexia, paralysis of the left arm, troubled vision, an intense nervous cough, and finally the patient's falling in love with her doctor. Anna O. gave Freud the evidence on which psychoanalysis was founded.

The characteristic of the scientific mind is the capacity to call in question data which to others seem nothing but ordinary everyday facts. Freud knew how to allow himself to be taken by surprise and had the openness to listen attentively to what the evidence had to tell him. If the 'talking cure' had been able to cure Anna O. of paralysis of the left arm and of her anorexia, it must mean that the human body can express a concrete human meaning through its functional abnormalities as well as by its conscious actions. Allowing itself to become the vehicle of thought in action, it itself becomes concrete speech. It is sufficient to accept factual data honestly, to read phenomena, as Husserl will say, to recognize the emptiness of the purely physiological scientific hypotheses which haunt the mind of man in our day, dominated as it is by a conception of the world which is based on technique. If the subject's talking was able to free her body, it must be because another talking, not spoken but lived, had in the first place bound it.

At one of his seminars Freud presented the object and originality of his work in a formula which is as sound as it is simple: 'To know the meaning of a phenomenon is much more interesting than to know the circumstances in which it has appeared... For us, this meaning is nothing but the purpose served by it (the faulty action) and the place occupied by it in the psychic series. We can even, in the greater number of our researches, replace the word "meaning" by the words "intention" or "tending".' One of the paragraphs of an encyclopaedia article published in 1922 is headed, 'Psychoanalysis as an Interpretative Art', and in justification of the method of free association, carried out by the patient and also by the psychoanalyst by reason of his listening with a free and floating attention, Freud wrote; 'In the first resort, this psychoanalysis was an art of *interpretation* and it sets itself the task of carrying deeper the first of Breuer's great discoveries—namely, that neurotic symptoms are significant substitutes for other mental acts which have been omitted. It was now a matter of regarding the material produced by the patients' associations as though it hinted at a hidden meaning and of discovering that meaning from it.'[1] Symptoms, therefore, express by proxy the truth which the patients' conscious speech has not been able to bring to birth.

Men are only themselves to the extent that they can express themselves; words of love, complaint, prayer, instruction, vindication are so many kinds of speech by which a man constitutes himself in human dignity. We understand with A. Malraux that art is a protest against fate and with Marx that social revolution is the sovereign act of assertion by which the proletariat overcomes that subservience with which it had entered into a servitude of connivance with its tyrants. In a quite different sphere, which would seem rather that of the caricature of man, Freud has surprised this same speech in the act of being born.

---

[1] *Standard Ed.*, XVIII, p. 239; *Collected Papers*, V, p. 111. It should be noted that *Absicht* should be translated 'intention' and not 'end'. 'Intention' indicates the developmental character of a tending which, even when unconscious, is of the order of consciousness.

Let us limit ourselves to the evidence provided by one dream, Dora's second dream after she started her treatment.[1] The classic imagery of the code of sexual symbolism is there in abundance—the railway station, the cemetery, the room, nymphs, the big book, the Madonna. But these are only dictionary words or signs in a rebus to be figured out. They bear within themselves possibilities of meaning. They are not indefinite, but neither are they definite, just as a word in a dictionary is rich with all the etymological and semantic sediment which has settled around it, but is itself not exhausted by it. Each expression receives its determination from the sentence in which it appears. But one sentence from a piece of writing, in its turn, does nothing but open up a field of possible meanings. No amount of linguistic study enables us to discern with precision the meaning of that diacritical sign we call a word. Every sign is within the intention which it embodies and at the same time beyond it, in so far as it opens up possibilities of meaning which the subject does not immediately realize. In the same way dream symbols, whether they are words or images, have to be interpreted, not read: they have to be figured out, not rendered by a word for word translation. Whence the extraordinary complexity of Freudian interpretations of dreams. During the sessions which followed Dora's second dream Freud came to recognize in it four levels of interpretation, indicated by four closely intertwined purposes. The situation which forms the façade of the dream is a fantasy of revenge directed against her father; then it can be seen that she has vengeful ideas against M. K., who is really the person disguised as her father; on the third level may be seen the love unconsciously entertained for this same M. K.; and at last, buried as deeply as it is in the hysterical symptoms, the homosexual attraction towards Mme K.

Pace certain practising psychologists and psychiatrists who

[1] 'Fragment of an Analysis of a Case of Hysteria', *Standard Ed.*, Vol. VII, p. 94.

harbour a nostalgia for a mechanical simplicity, a fifth level eventually arose out of these four levels of meaning, a fifth level that Freud did not recognize at the time, being still too anxious at this period to interpret himself the 'transference meaning of the dream.' By the way in which it disguised its meaning, the dream also revealed Dora's desire to revenge herself on her doctor, by discontinuing the treatment.[1] This calls for some explanation, because this fact takes us to the very heart of psychoanalysis, in so far as psychoanalysis is the interpretation of a meaning, symbolically expressed, and significantly substituted for mental acts not actually carried out.

Dora wished at one and the same time to be revenged on her father and on M. K., for motives which were partly the same and partly different. She also continued deep down to love M. K., on whom she had revenged herself when she had slapped his face and when she had refused to accompany him in the dream. But her love for M. K. was not the love of a woman for a man. Into this love had slipped her homosexual desire for Mme K. In her dream Dora goes through her own defloration in fantasy, but she puts herself in the position of the man who is penetrating her; she identifies herself with her admirer who lives abroad and it is really he who penetrates the thick wood on his way to the station. Her hate for M. K. is therefore doubly determined, it disguises her attraction towards him and at the same time expresses her jealousy with regard to Mme K. Her revenge on her father is also not far from the central motif of the dream; her father was in fact Mme K's lover, and so represented for Dora M. K.'s double. The four levels of meaning are constructed quite naturally one upon the other. But how, in this case, could the analyst miss this significant thread which draws the whole of the patient's situation together? For many reasons he reminded Dora of her father. And then through his work of interpreting he was relentlessly pursuing her in all

[1] *Ibid.*, p. 119.

the refuges of her symbolic ambiguities. There is no need to recall here all that Freud could have represented for his patient. It is enough briefly to indicate his place in the real life drama that Dora was living in front of him and with him. Among other things Freud represented for her the midwife who brings on the painful hour when truth is to be born. She cannot continue the psychoanalytic treatment without being brought to recognize her real intentions, which bear on her with such force that she has to express them in the figurative language of dreams. Only one solution can save her from having to see all her most private intentions brought out into the light of day—to break off the treatment. Dora's dream, while revealing the meaning of her illness, suggests by half-spoken words this ultimate strategem. At this period Freud was not sufficiently aware of the importance of the resistance, and of its meaning, to be a good listener. He could not lead his patient to see the meaning of her transference resistance. At this decisive point the treatment failed.

It is not surprising that after suffering an eclipse during the second analytic period (1900–1920), the idea of resistance reimposed itself on Freud with all its earlier insistence. Resistance shows that the disguising of the meanings which are made concrete in the symbols and symptoms is something positive. It therefore joins forces with the meaningful symptoms. It is because the symptoms have a meaning, or rather are a meaning, that they show resistance. They are the expression of the patient's private intention. The subject is projecting himself here as well as alienating himself. If it were not for this meaning expressed symbolically, he would go into a decline. Resistance to the demystification is at basis a healthy reaction of the personality as a whole against the danger of disintegration. In a sentence which is worth its weight in gold Freud wrote: 'The patient's symptoms constitute his sexual activity.'[1] A manifestation would not resist if

[1] 'My Views on the Part Played by Sexuality in the Aetiology of the Neuroses', *Standard Ed.*, Vol. VII, p. 278.

it was nothing but an accident on the fringe of the personality. A meaning deliberately made concrete is not a parasitic growth clinging to the personality, which could be cut away without in any way affecting the person's vital being.

It should be noted that 'meaning' and 'intention' do not in the least imply a conscious psychological state. They are the actual structures of willing and speaking and may or may not be integrated at the level of explicit consciousness. A historical incident, for example, may have a meaning, and obey a certain intentionality, even thought the intentionality may not be part of the concrete experience of the majority of the people who are making the history.

Dora really is this multiple intentionality that she is acting out in the web of her social relationships. She *is* these five levels of meaning expressed in dreams and actions. It is Freud's originality to have discovered, long before the pheno-menological psychologists, that a man does not carry his dreams and fantasies within him like pictures taken down from a wall,[1] but that he is this dreaming and imagining creature. A patient's symptoms *are* his sexual activity: they actualize his personal relationships.

Freud to some extent lacked philosophic terms with which to conceptualize his intuitions. But he was able to keep his thought from being contaminated by positivist psychology by forging dramatic terms which powerfully personified instincts and psychological conflicts.[2] His lengthy reflections on the relation between ideas and imagery on the one hand and affectivity on the other point to this same care to situate the meaning and description of a man's manifestations at the very heart of his being, which is desire and intention.

The path run by the development of the analytic technique practised by Freud has filled in the sketch of his first intention. He abandoned hypnosis because it ignores a man's need and

---

[1] This is Bergson's illustration of the imagination.
[2] See W. Muschg, 'Freud als Schriftsteller', in *Die psychoanalytische Bewegung*, II, 5, 1930.

right to resist, that is to say, to express as he understands it the meaning that he is able to actualize through his body and in his relationship with other people. For hypnosis Freud substituted interpretation, seeing the significance of the indications offered by the patient. The patient's own grasp of this significance, in a symbolic transference, has a cathartic effect because it makes a person open to representations and intentions which he is still refusing to accept and which nevertheless impose themselves on him with such insistence that he transforms them into bodily symbols, screen-images and faulty actions. But the psychoanalyst cannot with impunity impose his own interpretations on his patient. If for him 'every faulty action is a complete statement'[1] it is nevertheless necessary for the patient himself to verbalize this statement; anything else would be an act of violence and not a meaningful statement within the personal relationship of an authentic transference. Freud drew the logical conclusions from the evidence provided by the resistance and his method become less dictatorial.[2] He did not fall into the trap of continuing to attack some isolated farmhouse in which the enemy has stationed a deceptive resistance as a feint.[3] In resistance Freud was able to recognize the same meaning, the same intention, that was crying out to him in the other morbid manifestations.

The whole of Freud's efforts, then, are aimed at giving his central intuitions their full meaning. Psychoanalysis is the art

[1] J. Lacan, 'Fonction et champ de la parole et du langage en psychanalyse', in *La Psychanalyse*, Vol. I, p. 113.

[2] It is a misunderstanding of Freudian inspiration to say, 'It is necessary for someone else to interpret and to find out, so that I can be reconciled with myself. It is necessary for someone else to treat me as an object, as a field of causal excitation, and to regard even my consciousness as a symptom, as the effective sign of unconscious forces, so that I may recover my mastery over myself' (P. Ricœur, *Philosophie de la Volonté*, Vol. I, p. 361). There is no doubt that the Freud of the first period does lay himself open to such an interpretation, and that psychoanalysis does sometimes incline towards a determinism which is quite contrary to the directing ideas which guided Freud throughout his development.

[3] An illustration used by Freud in the *Interpretation of Dreams*.

of interpreting the meaning of psychological phenomena, that is to say, their tending or intention. This interpretation allows the mental acts for which the neurotic symptoms have been substituted, in virtue of their structural relationship, to be carried out. There is no room here to analyse all the aspects of these words, interpretation and meaning, and to relate them to the total of interpretations and meanings which appear in the related social sciences of the psychology of behaviour, history and linguistics. The meeting point of the social sciences is the primary interest which they all share in the expression of human meaning, whether by speech, by social institutions, or by behaviour. They have all come up against the problem of meaning, which is the point of their convergence, and the science which has taken as its task the elucidation of meaning as such is phenomenology.

Freud refused to enter into a dialogue with philosophy. His closest followers, however, have brought their thought into comparison with phenemenology. They realize that phenomenology is not a closed and definitive philosophy, a sort of Baedeker or *Guide Bleu* for living,[1] which would freeze all questions and betray that very capacity for asking them which is what constitutes man, that man with whom the psychiatrists also are concerned, as a being who engenders meaning.[2] Phenomenology is a return to the original intention of philosophy and so shares with psychoanalysis the concern to preserve and understand more deeply that power man has from Adam of naming things and of making meaningful relationships with other people. Let us first see, very briefly, how phenomenology is related to psychoanalysis and what contribution it can make to it. We will then delimit its field and establish the autonomy of psychoanalysis, which is sometimes threatened by irrelevant tentatives on

[1] This is what Freud thinks about philosophical systems.

[2] See Erwin Strauss, 'Man a questioning being' in *Tijdschrift voor Philosophie*, 1955. See also Dr H. Ey, *Études psychiatriques*, Vol. I, no. 2 and 3, and also his 'Introduction au traité de psychiatrie clinique et thérapeutique' in the *Encyclopédie médico-chirurgicale*, 1954.

the part of psychoanalysts as well as on that of phenome-
nalists.

II. Phenomenology and Psychology

In the philosophy of the man in the street phenomenology is
regarded as nothing more than a descriptive grasp of factual
data. Psychiatrists and psychologists are sometimes only too
pleased to take advantage of this presentation, which flatters
them in two ways: they come into the company of scholars
anointed with the prestige of philosophy, and they keep the
scientific key to their own inalienable domain, which phe-
menology has helped them to chart. For a descriptive technique only helps to throw into relief the enigmatic character
of mental illness; it can never provide an explanation. And
above all it does not oblige anybody to regard the phenomena in question as calling for an explanation, the meaning of which would then have to be considered.

But this would be a phenomenology based on the naturalistic
attitude: it is the very opposite of the philosophic attitude
that Husserl wants. Let us simply recall that the doctrine of
intentionality presented by Husserl in the *Logische Untersuchungen* was directed against the psychologism which was
reigning at the beginning of this century, a period so lacking
in true philosophy. Husserl reaffirms the autonomy of truth.
Truth exists in itself, even though seen through a plurality of
intentional acts, individualized by the number of subjects
and expressed in very different languages.

In the *Ideas* Husserl goes on to draw conclusions from the
nature of this intentional object. Its noetic correlate, the
subject who speaks and expresses himself, is not the empirical
subject of psychologism, subject to the laws of mental chemistry, but the transcendental subject directed towards objective
truth. The first phenomenological reduction, the eidetic
reduction, is a method of disengaging from concrete things
a pure essence which is independent of the person's original

intuition of the data and of the judgement he passes on that data. This reduction gives birth to engendering (*erzeugend*) intuition, which grasps the essence of the phenomena, their *eidos*. The intentionality of consciousness means that it is the presence of the essences that motivates the affirmation of a truth envisaged as more than empirical and it also means that the *eidos* comes into existence to complete an intended meaning. And then, with regard to constituted objects, the eidetic analysis studies the noematic correlates of the various modes of the constituting consciousness.[1]

Husserl's phenomenology, then, is not just the exploration of a field to be studied. It is a study of intentionality as the constituting act of consciousness, which posits meaningful structures and then grasps them in essential intuition. The expression, constitution, is very ambiguous as Husserl uses it. E. Fink[2] distinguishes many meanings—put together, put order into things, produce and complete; also, put order into our representations of things, and produce the meaning of the object out of the things which are presented to us in representations. But this continual sliding about of the meaning of constitution is a proof of Husserl's firm intention not to blunt the fine point of the intentionality of consciousness: this intentionality is both active and receptive, it constitutes meaning and contemplates it at the same time. This paradox is the very foundation of human consciousness, and will accompany Husserl in his ultimate attempt to seize this constitution of meaning at the very origin of the world.[3]

Whatever may be the ontological status of phenomenology, what matters here is that on all levels the phenomenological

---

[1] *Ideas*, § 92.

[2] Paper read at the *Colloque Phénoménologique de Royaumont*, April–May, 1957.

[3] This is the meaning of Husserl's tendency towards what has been called transcendental idealism, in so far as it appears in the *Ideas*. See the decisive article published by E. Fink with Husserl's complete approval, 'Die phänomenologische Philosophie E. Husserls in der gegenwärtigen Kritik' in *Kantstudien*, vol. 38, 1933.

reduction means the reversal of the naturalistic attitude; it means tracing constituted things back to their meaning as founded in their constitution. This movement, which is contrary to the naturalistic attitude, in which one gets bogged down in the matter-of-factness of the already-there, gives rise to a whole new ontology of speech and truth, and a whole existential analysis of the body, of the ego and of the world considered as the field of human endeavour.

We will not spend long on Heidegger's philosophy of speech. We just want to point out that this philosophy, continuing Husserl's concern to give language back its true nature as constituting meaning, is, from all the evidence, the ontological basis needed to make comprehensible Freud's intuition of illness as speech made concrete.[1] It should keep us from that continual illusion of wanting to look for the reality of the subject behind the wall of language and thinking that the truth of the subject is in the psychoanalyst, already given, and known by him in advance.[2] Freud, at every turn of his development, moved further and further away from a psychotherapy which would consist in pouring into the subject truths already possessed by the analyst.

An ontological reflection at Heidegger's level is certainly not indispensable. Freud got along very well without it. But he was brought up on the staple diet of European literature, and the poets, those prophets of authentic speech, wakened in him the echo of their own words. However, the danger of unphilosophic thought is that it may use philosophy without realizing it, and bad philosophy at that, with the obstinacy of a positivist standpoint which claims to submit itself to facts alone.

[1] In France it is the merit of Dr J. Lacan to have recentred psychoanalysis on speech. Helped by linguistics and ethnology and also by philosophy, Hegelian and that of Heidegger among others, he has given Freud's basic writings back their own dimension, that in which Freud himself situated his experience. See, in particular, the article in *La Psychanalyse, op. cit.*

[2] J. Lacan, *op. cit.*, p. 160.

The speech to which the psychoanalyst listens is in a very indirect language, that of imagery rooted in the living body, of functional troubles repeating the same theme in another mode, of faulty actions, eloquent like those of a sleepwalker in their embodiment of unadmitted intention. A Cartesian philosophy would not know what to do with these Freudian ideas! But since such a philosophy expresses and justifies the attitude of mind characteristic of a technical civilization, it permeates the atmosphere of all the sciences, affects the very conception of the arts and in psychologists and psychiatrists alike gives rise to working hypotheses which are blind to the real psychological nature of the phenomena Freud discovered. On this point also the renewal brought about by phenomenology, which has inspired the development to Gestalt psychology, should make it possible for the analytic discoveries to be fully exploited.

Attentive as always to the constitution of meaning, Husserl soon noticed the prime importance of the human body as the milieu of constitutive intentionality and as the field of the will.[1] Husserl compares language to a body: it is like the body of thought. 'The meant as such (*Meinung*) is not something external, residing in the words; on the contrary, in our speech we are all the time bringing to completion an internal intended meaning, which is based on the words but which at the same time animates them from within. The result of this animation is that the words and the speech as a whole embody an intention and that they carry within them this intention embodied as a meaning.'[2] It is within the body that intentionalities are engendered, and also the values by means of which man transforms the objects around him into the human world; his speech is also developed through the medium of the body. Speech then takes over and makes active in a socialized relationship the meaning already adum-

[1] See the excellent pages by P. Ricœur, *Philosophie de la Volonté*, I, pp. 116.
[2] *Formale und Transcendentale Logik*, p. 20.

brated through the body.[1] The whole of modern painting shows us that meaning, space and even time are immanent in the body, 'as it is conceived in the course of everyday life', according to the expression used by Descartes himself in one of his letters to Elizabeth (28.6.1643). Cézanne has discovered that in order to paint a look of sadness or a smile it is necessary to marry the colours in a certain way. But, he says, the devil if anyone ever realizes it!

Phenomenologists and Gestalt psychologists, then, have applied themselves to the study of the meanings which are engendered within the body, ambiguous and open to multifarious determinations, but nevertheless tracing vectors of possible meanings in which successive intentions can take form and existential reality. It is sufficient to draw attention to all the analyses of the different modes of conceiving space and time, and to the studies on the concept of the world, emotion as a magical kind of intention, the existential mode actualized by consciousness in weaving its fantasies and the sensations as organizers of meaningful wholes. Psychiatrists, psychologists and even biologists have been able to profit from this fund of philosophical riches; certain psychoanalysts as well, for example L. Binswanger, a close friend of Freud's, only too little known in France, very soon felt the similarity of inspiration in Freud's master ideas of time, the living body and language and the phenomenological current of thought. His attempt at synthesizing, which he calls *Daseinsanalyse* (existential analysis),[2] should certainly prove

[1] For the relationship between body and language, see also Merleau-Ponty, *Phénoménologie de la perception*, p. 203.

[2] See the two collections, *Ausgewählte Vorträge und Aufsätze*, I and II, Francke-Verlag, Bern, which include articles on phenomenology, Heidegger's analytics, the problem of language and thought, experience, understanding and interpretation in psychoanalysis, dreams, etc. Two important articles on the subject have just appeared in *Der Mensch in der Psychiatrie*, Pfullingen, 1957, one on man in psychiatry, the other 'my journey towards Freud'. M. Foucault has given us an important study of Binswanger by way of introduction to *Le Rêve et l'existence*, translated by J. Verdeaux.

of assistance to psychoanalytic research, provided it does not just use phenomenology or existential philosophy as a parameter with regard to analytic experience. Following the same line of thought E. von Gebsattel[1] has written some illuminating pages on obsessional organizations of space and time, and on the constitution of the psyche in relation to multiple personality, etc.

The danger of a psychoanalysis which tries to be purely empirical is that it will philosophize without realizing it. The concepts used by Freud and his followers all carry a hidden charge of anthropology. It is too easily forgotten that Freud, gifted as he was with an exceptional capacity for asking questions, gave a new meaning to the psychological concepts which permeated his cultural background. Phenomenology is not a substitute for the disciplines of the natural and social sciences, but it helps them to 'understand their own productions in as much as the intentionality which produces them remains in them in an implicit state.'[2] It analyses the philosophy which is implicit in every scientific theory and in all scientific research. In so doing phenomenology exorcizes from the sciences the myths which envelop them and obscure their field of vision.

It is only necessary to look at some of the key concepts of contemporary psychoanalysis to realize the weight of naturalism under which Freud's original intuitions are being crushed. Dream symbols are often explained as if they were mass-produced statues, quite separate from the context of living relationship which they symbolize and at the same time punctuate. And the whole relationship of the subject to his world is sometimes enclosed in the curve of a graph showing his adaptation towards the object and his integration of the object. People do not seem to realize that even in experimental psychology the formalist concept of homeostasis is accepted in its fundamental ambiguity. The object of study

---

[1] *Prolegomena einer medizinschen Anthropologie*, 1954.
[2] *Formale und Transcendentale Logik*, p. 12.

in perception is not the causal interaction of a subject and an object but the actual organization of the immediate environment by the perception, because this also expresses the nucleus of the perceiving subject.[1]

A phenomenological critique will also protect psychoanalysis from a hardening of the concepts of language and body, and will help it to arrive at a synthesis between these two modes of expression, which are always in a state of continual interdependence and interchange. The living body is animated by an intention which makes it human and confers on it its symbolic function. And it is because it is not frozen in its materiality that the cathartic word can descend into it, modify the form which animates it and confer on it a new symbolic function.[2] Speech itself is engendered within an intention which can only come to completion by means of the quasi-materiality of spoken language, but which nevertheless remains always beyond it. And this intention goes through the body before crystallizing into speech. It takes root in the concrete experience mediated by the body, without which it would be pure form, and itself takes on the weight of reality when it can no longer animate it; the materialized speech of schizophrenics can be referred to indifferently as material or as purely formal.

To summarize. Phenomenology, while jealously keeping all noematic data in an intentional correlation with a noesis, has carried out a basic critique of all naturalistic thought concerning language, the body, freedom and the emotions. It locates thought at the very centre of the intended meaning and allows it to grasp at their source all the ambiguities with

[1] See J. Nuttin, *Tâche, réussite et échec. Théorie de la conduite humaine*, p. 89.

[2] In Paris Dr F. Dolto, in particular, has developed this idea of the symbolic mediation of the living body in a man's relationship with other men and with the world. Cf. *Psychanalyse et pédiatrie*, 1940. Within the same line of thought Dr Pankow has published a critical study of the treatment of two cases of schizophrenia, which was based on the patients' becoming aware of the fundamental structure of their bodily system, *Structuration dynamique dans la schizophrénie*, Huber, Bern, 1956.

which the psychoanalyst finds himself daily confronted—
symbolic imagery continually turning into its opposite, conflicting motives based on each other, the conception of the
body continually destroyed and reformed. Phenomenology
gives form to the schemata which emerge from analytic experience. It does not, however, supplant the latter. And it is
no less necessary to insist briefly on the opposite side of the
relationship between psychoanalysis and phenomenology.

The Relationship between Phenomenology and the Irreducible Autonomy of the Analytic Experience

Some phenomenologists have felt threatened by psychoanalysis because it maintains the irreducibility of the idea of
the unconscious. Summarizing the views of Sartre, who himself echoes G. Politzer, Fr Jeanson writes: 'The phenomenological task would lose all meaning if there existed a psychic
unconscious.'[1] On the other hand, however, some people
find in phenomenology a way of escaping from the real point
of the Freudian discovery. On the level of immediate phenomena, phenomenology furnishes them with the tools necessary for understanding what the mentally ill person is doing
and enables them to bring their language into line with the
basic laws of linguistics, etc. But they remain convinced anti-
analysts because they refuse to go beyond this first step of
the eidetic reduction.[2] Fundamentally they do not see that
the meaning engendered by man is so much the foundation
of his personality that this meaning necessarily becomes concrete, woven out of question and conflicts, tending towards
neurosis, somtimes getting frozen and sometimes freeing itself
by gaining access to a new concretely lived meaning.

A static transverse section of the patient's mind, as it is
practised by some people with the help of eidetic analysis,

---

[1] *La Phénoménologie*, 1951, p. 87.
[2] The whole of Husserl's criticism of naturalism in psychology is also
valid against this current of thought. See *Erste Philosophie* I, p. 51.

is a misunderstanding of this basic concreteness—imagery, actions, behaviour and language—which characterizes man in all his being. This concreteness is by its nature dialectic: it progresses by negation and integration. Phenomenology in so far as it is a study of meaning should therefore be essentially concrete: as Sinngenesis says, it does not deal with eternal ideas but with the origin of meaning.[1]

The intentional account of man does not exclude factual data, such as concrete events and biological and hereditary factors. Freud always insisted on the biological conditioning of mental illness. But neither the web of events, nor a man's biological constitution, are ever anything more than motivating factors, taken up into an intentional plan which affirms them, challenges them and goes beyond them. A concretely lived meaning can never be reduced to a mere indication of something other than itself, whether that something is a historical event or a biological factor. Anecdotal psychoanalysis is nothing but a caricature.

At the other extreme existential analysis, by getting rid of unconscious intentionality, is unfaithful both to Freud and to phenomenology. If on the ontological level Husserl dreams of making all the operational concepts of philosophy transparent and of going back to the original ground (*Urstiftung*) which would coincide with the ultimate ground (*Endstiftung*), on the level of the social sciences he has come to realize more and more the futility of his original plan of disengaging by means of reduction a logic and linguistics which would be universal and absolute. Phenomenology ought to place itself at the very heart of the various disciplines and elucidate them from within, whether it is a matter of history, psychology, linguistics or physics. To prejudge the psychological unconscious by starting from descriptions of present consciousness leads then to an encounter with phenomenology as well as with psychology. Because, however obscure this idea may still be at the present state of analysis, Freud made it the

[1] 'Philosophie als Strenge Wissenschaft' in *Logos*, I, 1910, p. 338.

corner stone of his technique of interpretation and of his understanding of human lives. No doubt to a certain extent he overlooked the depth of the subject's conscious intentions, and M. Scheler's criticism in this regard retains all its usefulness.[1] One of the tasks of a psychoanalysis enriched by a more authentic philosophy would be to study the dialectical relationship between consciousness and the unconscious in the light of this idea of the foundation of meaning, central both to Freud's thought and to contemporary philosophy.

All these critical reflections are not strictly indispensable. But it is obvious that in one way or another every scientist tends to elucidate and systematize the operational concepts which obscurely animate his intuitions and his working hypothesis. Moreover, in this spontaneous philosophy, the capacity for asking questions which Freud brought to light is directed towards the most obscure regions of man's make-up. What could be more faithful to the founder of psychoanalysis than to set in action by critical reflection this gleam of truth which is born with man's first action and his first words? And what could be more human? 'Denn das fragen ist die Frömmigkeit des Denkens.'[2]

[1] *The Nature of Sympathy*, London, 1954, p. 196.
[2] Heidegger, *Vorträge und Aufsätze*, p. 44.

A VERY OLD IDEA AND SOME OTHERS WHICH ARE NOT SO OLD

Dr Paul Cossa

Most people of my generation learnt that there was some-thing called conscience, a spontaneous disposition to judge our own actions, and above all other people's, because, good beggars that we are, we keep the front pocket of our beggar's scrip for the motes out of our brother's eye and only too readily throw towards the back pocket the beams which have made ourselves half-blind.

The modern schools of psychology, psychoanalytic as well as behaviourist, have crossed the idea of conscience out of their vocabulary: it is too highly charged with subjectivism, they say, and so cannot be observed from outside, and cannot be expressed in terms of behaviour; it is too highly charged, also, with metaphysical elements and presupposes a belief in the spiritual.[1]

It is necessary, however, to admit the existence of some-thing in ourselves, some power or function which opposes our instinctive tendencies, in order to account for the conflicts aroused in us by our actions and even by our desires. This something is envisaged differently by the different psycho-analytic schools.

We know that Freud's original view simply opposed our instinctual demands to the constraints of the external world.

[1] Not to mention the difference in moral criteria; for example in sexual matters bourgeois morality has nothing in common with Christian morals.

However, he soon realized that some of the childhood sexual traumas revealed by analysis had never actually taken place, and that they were imaginative inventions on the part of the patient. And so he realised that neurosis is not caused by actual happenings, by the external world giving rise to conflicts in childhood, but that it is due to the idea of the outside world the child has built up for himself; Freud isolated this idea of the outside world, in which he saw nothing but the introjection of social imperatives, and regarded it as a particular autonomous function or mental agency. He named it the superego (*Überich*). It is the clash between all the instinctive impulses (*Triebe*), basically sexual, which he calls libido, and this superego, which gives rise to the initial conflict. What follows on from this—the repression of the conflict and the part played by this repression in the genesis of neurosis—need not be gone into in detail. Let us just recall that all the psychological material susceptible of being repressed constituted for Freud another agency of the mind, the id (*das Es*).

Ego, superego, id—without mentioning the libido—are thus three entities, three concepts isolated by Freud at this stage of his doctrinal development. Everyone knows that afterwards his thought took an even more dogmatic turn, with the distinction of the *Ichtriebe* as tendencies within the libido with the same status as the *Sexualtriebe*, the introduction of narcissism, the emphasis on the fundamental aggressiveness of the young child, and finally the reduction of the whole problem to a Manichean opposition between Eros and Thanatos.

To the mental agencies isolated by Freud, Jung added others. His conception of the ego is more or less that of Freud, but what he calls the shadow does not coincide completely with the id. By the shadow Jung means not so much what is repressible as what is repressed, what we refuse to allow into consciousness. In the same way, the persona is related to the superego; but it takes on the more precise meaning of a social mask, a false personality impressed on the individual by his social conformity. As to the self (*das Selbst*), this is the personality ideal towards which the individual is tending.

So Freud enumerates three mental agencies, and Jung four: but Stocker admits three more, Desoille four, and Baudouin adds one more, the automaton. These variations are enough to show that inventions of this kind can easily bring in an element of artificiality, just as the old idea of conscience was taxed with verbalism; and here we are with fresh ideas being constructed, which are nothing but exercises of the imagination, to the number of three or four, or even eight or ten if account is taken of the shades of meaning which prevent, for example, the identification of the shadow and the id.

It cannot be too much emphasized that these conceptions, or at least Freud's, presuppose a basic metaphysical position: to regard the superego as the only check on the instincts, and to say that it is nothing but the introjection of social imperatives, is to assume in principle that there is nothing in man but instincts, which are biological, and the reaction of these instincts to the external world, which is also biological. This is a profession of materialism and metaphysical sociology similar to that of Durckheim.[1]

[1] It is only fair to point out that among those who maintain this bio-sociological position not all are materialist to the same extent. Freud was, Durckheim certainly less so, since he admitted a kind of spiritualization by the social situation, this spiritual aspect arising out of society considered as a synthesis and not as the totality of individuals. But a belief in the spiritual is more demanding. It requires that the good, the beautiful and conscience should all be regarded as manifestations of the spiritual. It could not adopt the bio-sociological position without supposing a secondary intervention during the development towards adulthood, a transcendent intervention by spirit, come in its own interests to take over the psyche, and this would be even more dualist than Descartes.

Fortunately the adherents of the bio-sociological position have in no way proved that spirit does not exist, or that it does not intervene in the genesis of conscience. They have only said so, and there is no scientific reason why those who accept the existence of the spiritual should take their word for it.

It is amusing to see those who accuse the defenders of conscience of writing metaphysics doing the same thing in their turn, so difficult is it to push the analysis of anything to its logical conclusion without entering into metaphysics, which tries to define natures and essences.

A second criticism of these ideas should be made: the most important contribution to psychopathology made by the psychoanalytic schools, and in the first place by Freud, is certainly the idea that neurosis arises out of an unconscious conflict. Now, to speak of conflict implies the existence of opposing forces. We are acquainted with one of those forces, the instinctive impulses, whether or not they are christened libido. But what, then, is the opposition?

Once Freud had seen what was wrong with his first approach, he answered, 'the superego, that is to say the idea of the outside world that the child constructs for himself.' Jung tells us, 'it is the persona', that is to say the idea of his own personality fashioned by the child under the pressure of social conformity.

And so, it seems, these writers envisage a conflict between a real force on one side, that is the instinctive impulses, and, on the other side—what? An idea. No doubt a terrifying, constraining, coercive idea, but an idea all the same. Can one really envisage a fight between a projectile and a shadow?

For social prohibitions and commands to be able to impress the child with such an intensity as to counterbalance the living forces of his instincts, something else is surely necessary: these prohibitions must find an echo of deep agreement in the child, they must awaken other forces, as live, as deep, as securely rooted in the individual as are those of instinct.[1]

[1] If an individual lacks this internal force, would social prohibitions and commands manage to break these instinctive impulses? The answer is no. Such people—they are well known to psychopathology—are untroubled by any anxiety or feeling of guilt on account of their failure to conform socially; they flout rules and know how to do so with impunity; they feel no anger, but often, on the contrary, show a sporting admiration

Neither Freud nor his followers have overlooked this difficulty. Freud tried to solve it in the first place by setting *Sexualtriebe* and *Ichtriebe* in opposition; he then brought in narcissism
in opposition to instinct and ended up by locating the conflict between Eros and Thanatos. By their very variation
these doctrines incline to the mythical and do not offer much
credibility. Some of his followers have seen the principal
cause of anxiety, and so of the feeling of duty, in the instinct
of self-preservation.[1]

But this idea leads to an impasse; even in everyday life
there are occasions when the instinct of self-preservation and
the sense of duty are in conflict, and there are cases in which
the former gives way completely to the latter—the deliberate
sacrifice of a railwayman who saves a child from a train. If
the sense of duty were really only a by-product of the instinct
of self-preservation, how could it ever overcome it? Does an
instinct destroy itself?

It so happens that the old idea of conscience, provided we
are not content to consider it as a whole but are prepared to
separate it into its constituent elements, allows us to define
the forces opposed to instinct quite clearly, and in a way, we
think, which should not disturb any philosophical belief.

Moral philosophy distinguishes two things in conscience—
the dictate and the content:

for the representative of the law. Everyone has known children whom
no authority, no method, has been able to control, seducers of young
girls who manage to evade all disagreeable consequences, swindlers whom
no investigation can manage to nail down; these people are without
remorse or anxiety; they do not have neuroses.

[1] At the beginning of his development the child is punished by someone
in his social environment if he breaks a rule. Very soon the desire to
break a rule is outweighed by the fear of punishment. To avoid punishment he even avoids intending to break the rules. In all this—flight from
punishment, flight from the fear of punishment—he is obeying the instinct of self-preservation. This attitude, however, is not submission to
the external world. And the feeling of frustration in its turn gives rise to
anxiety and humiliation. To avoid this, the child deludes himself; he
interiorizes the suffered constraint. He has not given in to external
pressure, but to internal pressure, and this internal pressure he calls duty.

1. *The dictate* is the innate disposition to judge and to judge oneself, to justify oneself to oneself as well as to judge someone else.

This need exists at least in an embroyonic state[1] in the small child; it can be found, according to Baruk, in the insane; it is anchored in the innermost depths of the human being.

One does not have to believe in the spiritual to accept this notion. The believer may certainly see in this function a gift of God, the voice of God, and nothing prevents him from thinking that if the voice of God finds such an echo in himself it is because it corresponds to an instinct. But the materialist, for his part, may regard this need that we have called a dictate as being only an instinct,[2] of purely organic origin. Is this any more difficult for him than to see, as he often does, the sublimated manifestation of another instinct in the most exalted expressions of charity? To accept this dictate as a fact will not hurt his philosophic beliefs any more than accepting the fact of charity.

2. *The content,* or, as we should prefer to say, the criteria, of conscience. The dictate remains in us without changing, but the criteria of our judgement differ considerably in our development from birth to adulthood. Let us take an example:— one should not over-eat. The baby knows that the end of his feed is indicated by the removal of his bottle: the child remembers past stomach-aches; the adolescent or the adult

---

[1] It may be objected that the dictate of conscience does not always appear very clearly in the child; and certainly the child may very easily confuse the instructions of the outside world and those of his *daemon.* In just the same way, when he becomes capable of grasping his foot in both hands, he is still unable to distinguish it from the surrounding objects and to see that it is a part of himself. But the disposition is no less innate because it does not materialize immediately. As an adolescent's sudden passion for music on attending his first concert is only the deferred appearance of an innate gift.

[2] And why not a manifestation of the herd instinct, urging him to submit to the law of the clan?

knows that too much food, and in particular too much alcohol, interferes with the freedom of the intellect, and even with that of the spiritual life.

So, from the earliest age to the adult state, one same virtue, that of temperance, goes through three successive types of motivation: one, the end of the meal, imposed by the environment; the second, memory of stomach-aches, imposed by physiology; the third, ethical ideas, freely accepted by the moral being.

In the development of the individual these three types of motivation succeed each other but do not completely replace each other. But just as in neurology the more recently acquired functions take priority over the older ones, so the more recent types of motivation tend to take priority over the preceding ones. This is known as Jackson's Law. If the fully developed adult is not a glutton, this may be solely due to the virtue of temperance; he no longer needs to remember his childhood stomach-aches, even less the prohibitions of his earliest training.

But how many of us adults can boast of being completely developed?

Very few, I am afraid; most of us have not been able to get rid of the archaic motivation of our earliest parental training; most of us have been unable to liquidate the taboos and bogies of childhood. And so we can distinguish two kinds of motive for our actions: one kind perpetuates in our adult life the impulses and prohibitions of childhood. We do not admit their existence to ourselves. The other kind, fully conscious, expresses the criteria of our adult conscience. Often they are nothing more than a cover for the former. A man of considerable intellectual capacity may be spending an excessive amount of time in local politics, to the great detriment of his intellectual and spiritual life. In his own eyes he is sacrificing himself to his duty as an important person; an analysis would show him that in fact he was obeying an unconscious desire to compensate himself for the humiliations of his childhood as the son of a servant.[1]

Here again in this idea of the content of conscience we do not see anything which could hurt anyone's philosophical beliefs: no follower of Freud will have any difficulty in accepting that the content of conscience comes from the external world.

The believer in the spiritual has no difficulty either: is he not covered by St Thomas': 'nihil est in intellectu quod nisi prius in sensu'?[2]

Is it possible, starting from these ideas, to give a consistent account of what may be psychogenetic in the mechanism of the neuroses? We think it could be put rather like this:

conflict is habitual to the childhood psyche;

conflicts arises between instinctive impulses, on the one hand, whatever they may actually be,[3] and on the other hand, this personal imperative which enables the person to appreciate the social compulsions and prohibitions he experiences in the form in which he is able to grasp them.

If this starting point is once accepted—and it is only, under a different formulation, what all the present psychogenetic schools accept—the various elements of psychogenesis may be admitted or rejected as each one likes: whether or not primacy should be given to the sexual; whether the conflict

[1] The first idea the child forms of the external world, of its compulsions and its prohibitions, provides the first nourishment for the dictate and the first content for the conscience. Just because it satisfies a powerful tendency, a real appetite, it makes a deep impression on the childhood psyche. By the nature of things this idea is reduced to the child's vision, and is distorted. And it is this distortion which makes it dangerous. This distortion should be minimized as far as possible, and no room should be found for taboos and bogies. For this it will be necessary to reform educational ideas and to bring moral ideas into line. It should not be forgotten that, according to Sears, the famous Freudian castration complex is not found amoung young people who, as children, have had a sensible sexual education.

[2] There is no intellectual principle which has not been initiated by some sensory experience.

[3] Whether sexual or not.

should be limited to childhood, or, in accordance with what seems to us the very important contribution made by Jung, the possibility of conflicts capable of giving rise to a neurosis in adolescents and adults should be admitted; the part played by emotional immaturity, whether this is due to the original conflict or to a constitutional predisposition; toleration of the conflict so long as the subject's age or circumstances make it possible for him not to face it; when this is no longer possible, refuge in illness, which is a childish reaction, explained by emotional immaturity; in brief a general idea of neurosis as a defence, by flight against aggression, internal or external, which may give rise to anxiety on the part of a psyche which is insufficiently armed or has been disarmed. There is nothing in all this which cannot be fitted in with the idea of an initial conflict, as it has been described above.[1]

Here, the *daemon* intervenes: 'my son, you have pleaded for simplicity. But are you sure that you are really representing things as they are? Are you sure you are not being deceived by the turn of your own mind? A certain succinct—and Latin—taste for simplification? A disinclination to admit that truth may be complex?'

But why should not the truth be simple? Has not Freud himself admitted as much in the last, and dualist, formulation of his doctrine? In any case, is it forbidden to formulate complex things simply? Hamlet has taught us that there are more things in heaven and earth than the human mind can conceive of, and more things in one human mind than that mind can express. But it is not overlooking the complexity of facts to disengage the essential from them, and to emphasize this essential by formulating it simply.

And yet, is your view right, are you quite sure? Does it follow strictly from the facts? And does not this obstinacy in defending an ancient formula point to preoccupations which

---

[1] To formulate it in another way: between the instinctive impulses and the earliest content of the conscience, activated by the dictate; between instincts and bogies.

are not purely scientific? When all is said and done, are you not writing metaphysics?

But who is being the more metaphysical? The theory that I am refuting can only be accepted by a materialist; it is true that the theory I have set out above is in conformity with the spiritual tradition, but a materialist could accept it. Is the fact that it fits in with my belief a good reason for rejecting it?

This agreement between a philosophy and a psychological theory would certainly seem suspect if the theory had no other basis. But the statements of fact are there, and the personality of the one who first draws them up is a convincing surety for himself alone. Where did I start from? From the fact of conflict. The second force, the second combatant should not be looked for outside the subject, in the external world, but inside the subject himself, in the hidden depths of his own psyche. But this statement is not mine. It comes from Freud himself. It is the last phase of his thought. It is true that he called this force Thanatos, setting it over against the libido or Eros: death against sex, the desire to die against the desire to live. If one does not accept the myth, must one also reject the statement of fact which gave rise to it? And in order to explain this statement of fact, is it forbidden to go back to a traditional and no less empirical conception of the conflict which tears human nature, and to say: 'the desire which comes from the flesh against the desire which comes from the spirit'?

THE PSYCHOANALYST AND THE
CONFESSOR

Marc Oraison

Doctor of Theology, Doctor of Medicine

It seems that the tower of Pisa, leaning dangerously on its foundations, is causing anxiety among architects and the responsible authorities. They have no wish to see it fall down, and they are examining the point where the foundations meet the ground, in the hope of finding the cause, probably complex, of this excessive disequilibrium. It does not occur to anybody to suppose that it is due to lack of light, and to suggest an atmospheric super-ventilator to disperse the clouds which are getting in the way of the sun, or, worse still, the construction of an artificial source of light as powerful as possible as a sort of substitute for the sun.

However, it is just such a mental feat which, *mutatis mutandis*, is being indulged in in another field, when certain well-intentioned writers say that frequent confession under a good director should lead to the cure of neurosis. Remarks such as the following are still being heard far too often: 'what is the good of psychoanalysis, since we have confession? In confession a man unburdens his soul of everything which is weighing it down; what need has he to talk to somebody other than his confessor?' Or again it is pointed out, not incorrectly, as a matter of fact, that psychoanalysis has spread much more widely in protestant countries, where there is no confession, than in catholic countries where it is the custom. However, this means nothing: it is quite possible that confession answers one need and psychoanalysis another, and

that protestant countries have fallen into the opposite confusion from the one to which we have just drawn attention
and that they find in psychoanalysis an inadequate substitute
for confession.

It must be said that remarks of this kind point to an almost
complete ignorance of the nature of psychoanalysis, which is
a medical activity, and also to a serious misunderstanding of
the nature of confession, which is a religious and sacramental
activity.

It is time something was done to clear up this confusion,
which is systematically maintained, for widely differing reasons which are irrelevant here, even by some writers who call
themselves theologians. It would of course be childishly pre-
tentious to imagine that an exhaustive and definitive criticism
could be carried out in a dozen pages, but a few remarks or
clarifications may give the reader some means of discrimi-
nating for himself. This is the aim of the present chapter.

Briefly, psychoanalysis and confession are two techniques,
both at the service of man. That is to say, they both aim at
promoting his good: a deeper, clearer, and more unselfish
integration into the life of relationship. But these two techniques are situated at radically different levels: in Pascal's
sense of the term, they are not of the same order. As we said
at the beginning, psychoanalysis as such is a medical activity,
whereas confession as such is a religious activity. This introductory distinction, elementary as it is, is already charged
with meaning.

Everybody knows that the psychoanalyst is concerned with
his client's unconscious, but people are rather vague as to
what this really means. This is understandable: our mentality,
that is to say our habit of thinking, is still too strongly affected
by rationalism to be at ease with fluid realities which are
grasped only with difficulty and escape the net of abstract and
definitive concepts, and which can be expressed much better
by means of symbols than by syllogistic reasoning.

A man's unconscious world is rather like the mysterious underground formation, obscure and vaguely threatening, which makes it possible for the river to spring out of the cliff at the Fontaine de Vaucluse. It is not known exactly what goes on there; there are intuitions, indications, hypotheses; it is not possible adequately to formulate these obscurely glimpsed fluid realities by means of a vocabulary adapted to the expression of clear ideas; and that is the only vocabulary we have. But we know also that this underground formation, however different it may be from the gleam of light playing on the springing waters, unquestionably has a part to play in that dynamism by which these waters so wonderfully spring forth.

It is of the nature of the unconscious to be irrational. Or, more precisely, sub-rational. To use the Freudian language, it may be said, a little schematically, to correspond to un-resolved emotional complications left over from the pre-rational period of childhood. For man begins his existence in the mystery of protean shadows, even though Revelation teaches us that grace brings his restlessness to an end in the mystery of the divine light. The psychoanalyst is only con-cerned with this mystery of shadows, and to the extent that its persistence is harmful. All neurotic troubles, whether serious or slight, are rooted in this mystery. The small child's instinctive actions and emotional reactions express the first hesitating encounter of his individuality with the outside world, both inert and human. It may happen that this encounter, intensely experienced in a way that is still purely affective, involves conflicts too heavy for him to bear. It may be that the almost physical anxiety that he experienced in such and such circumstances was not sufficiently dispersed at the time. This anxiety, strenuously forgotten by a sort of defence mechanism, will remain unconsciously seething and always ready to reappear. The psychoanalyst's job is simply to help his patient recognize this underlying anxiety, which the treatment leads him in a way to live over again in the consulting room. This is the only way the subject himself can disperse it; as he relives it, he sees it, so to speak, as archaic and without any cause in the present.

That is to say, the psychoanalyst only deals with the infra-human zone in his patient. Analytic treatment proceeds only on this level. His aim is to free his patient, not as some people believe, and would have it believed, in relation to moral principles, but in relation to his paralysing anxiety, which is characterized precisely by having no connection with moral purposes. In brief, the only concern is with those first babblings, not yet outlived, which the subject made when he first entered into an instinctive dialogue with the world outside, his first attempt, still purely emotional, at the life of relationship.

As against this, the confessor is concerned, if one may express it in this way, with the highest level of life in the person who has recourse to him that one can possibly think of. His place is at the opposite extreme to that of the psychoanalyst: he re-establishes, or confirms, although in a purely instrumental manner, the person's life in the supernatural dimension which is its highest reach: his personal relationship with God his Saviour. We are here at the opposite extreme of the human mystery, at the supreme achievement of his life of relationship, made possible by grace, that is to say, by the free and superabounding gift of God, known as Infinite Love. There is no longer question, strictly speaking, of psychology, but rather of that transcendent and ineffable mode of knowledge which we call faith. If the part of the psyche with which the psychoanalyst is concerned may be specifically described as obscure and subterranean, we are here, on the contrary, in the most perfect dazzling light, so dazzling for our limited and hesitating minds that it blinds us all as it sweeps us into its whirlwind of brightness and gives us the hope of life. And that is why a clinical psychology of faith, unlike the speculative and rational study elaborated by theology, remains in principle impossible: its manifestations may be studied and even re-orientated, but its essence can never be defined. Any more than Montaigne, when he was asked about his friendship with La Boétie, could explain further than, 'because he is himself, and I am myself'. It seems unquestionable that the misuse of a legalistic vocabulary and the effect of a legalistic mentality only too often leads to its being forgotten that the sacrament of penance is situated essentially in a personal relationship: man wandering and wounded, and God following him with tenderness (Osee), trying to rouse him from his apathy (Canticle of Canticles), and welcoming him with a grand and overflowing demonstration of love when he returns (the Prodigal Son). Rational explanation is no longer possible here; it is the very mystery of living love, of that recognition between two persons, the inexpressible that passed between Christ and Peter after Peter's denial, when they exchanged that glance recorded by Saint Luke. God calls each of us by name, and that is what gives us our existence; he saves each of us by name: 'because he is himself and I am myself'. In this supreme dialogue of rediscovered friendship with God the confessor is nothing but an instrument; because this friendship, freely and superabundantly given on the part of God, manifests itself to our knowledge by concrete signs: Scripture, the living history of the revelation of this friendship, and the sacraments, at the same time its expression and its reality.

One should beware of certain ambiguous expressions which can easily be misunderstood if it is forgotten that they were originally intended to be metaphorical. Such is the case with transposed medical language: sin, the sickness of the soul; the confessor, doctor of souls, etc. There is, no doubt, an analogy in the sense that in sin as in physical illness there is a disturbed harmony, a disturbance in vital function. But all the same the infinite distance which separates these two levels should not be lost from view. A few years ago a theologian who is very strongly opposed to Freudian psychoanalysis, writing about the spiritual life in a review which fortunately does not have a very large circulation, said: 'the spiritual life is a higher unconscious'. This is a good example of the sort of nonsense which can lead to serious confusion. The unconscious is a chaotic and prehistoric world which precedes or underlies conscious life; the life of grace, is, on the contrary, that all-powerful force of the divine friendship which mobilizes, takes up and unifies beyond their own limits, in faith, all the rational forces of consciousness.

During the course of psychoanalytic treatment the psychoanalyst and his patient move at the level of the infra-rational and the infra-human, since the need is precisely to disengage the rational and the human from the archaic quicksands which are impeding it. In the liturgical and mysterious encounter of the sacrament, the confessor and his penitent move at the level of the supra-rational and of the supernatural strictly so-called. If one may put it this way, the psychoanalyst and the confessor are situated at the two opposite extremes of the dynamic unity of the human person.

This fundamental difference of order and of nature between confession and psychoanalysis involves a no less fundamental difference between the method and attitude of the confessor and those of the analyst.

The confessor, situated, if one may say so, at the point of an encounter between two people in a court of law—the penitent and God—is called upon in a certain way to pass judgement. But it must not be lost from view that this judgement is a particular sort of judgement, and the very ambiguous comparison often made between this and a judgement of human justice runs the risk of falsifying the perspective. It follows that the customary expression 'the tribunal of penance' leads to the danger of confusion, which is a serious matter from the point of view of sound religious doctrine.

This is in fact the only tribunal at which a person presents himself with the absolute certainty of being pardoned the moment he asks. The gospel on each occasion emphasizes not so much the legal aspect of judgement as that of a warm welcome for the wanderer: the parable of the Prodigal Son, Mary Magdalen the sinner, the Samaritan woman. During the course of centuries the idea of the sacrament of penance has no doubt been influenced by the legislation of the visible ecclesiastical body, which for the good of the community needs a juridical and procedural organization of the same type as that of civil justice. For example the public sinner, divorced and remarried in open defiance of the Christian view of marriage, is visibly excluded from the community, that is to say from participation at the table around which the faithful assemble for the eucharistic meal. But the secret and personal relationship of each one with God is not of the same order and the legalism which is necessary in the visible organization of the temporal community should not affect our conception of the sacrament in itself. It can serve only as a comparison, or more precisely as an analogy, and not as an adequate description. The priest as such, that is as minister of the sacrament, instrument of the mystery, may be compared not so much with a judge as with the nameless gatekeeper of the father who awaits the return of the prodigal son, ready to celebrate the reunion with a feast.

Nevertheless he has a judgement to make, because he is not a mechanical instrument; he is given a mission by the Church which calls for the engagement of all his human faculties as well as his spiritual disposition and the supernatural power which is entrusted to him. He is going to give something in the name of God, a sign which is at the same time efficacious of grace; that is to say a gift whose value is incalculable and of primary importance to the penitent who is waiting for it and asking for it. As the dispenser of this gift the priest has to judge whether there is occasion to give it. That is to say, it is necessary for him to know in the first place if there is a penitent, that is to say if the person presenting himself, in this essentially transcendent personal relationship, is really a sinner: whence the need for the confession of sins.

Then he has to assure himself that the person knows what he is doing, that is to say, that he has the necessary disposition of repentance and faith, that the act which he is making is truly a religious act and not just thought of as a more or less magical rite, or as an exercise conducive to his natural well-being; whence the need for the penitent to indicate his contrition. But the judgement of the confessor goes no further than this—the confession of sins, contrition, firm purpose of amendment, according to the traditional formula. It is quite clear that the confessor can in no sense judge the deep personal responsibility of the penitent: that is something for God alone. He may point out that a particular action is grave in itself and say why, but he cannot attempt to settle the question of what is called in traditional theology the formal responsibility of the person who is talking to him without making a dizzy and outrageous mistake.[1] That would be clericalism, not priesthood. If the priest in this supernatural encounter of confession has to pass a judgement, he should not forget that this judgement must remain within the framework of his own capacity: that is to dispense the infinite mercy which surpasses him just as much as it surpasses his penitent.

With the psychoanalyst it is quite the opposite; if he is faithful to the exigencies of his method he will meticulously refrain from passing any value judgement on his patient's behaviour, for the very simple reason that his intervention takes place at the level of the infra-human, and therefore infra-moral zone. All he does, which does not mean that it will be easy or rapid, is to help someone who is mentally ill to discover in himself those emotional charges of archaic origin which, blocked and under pressure, are shackling to a greater or lesser degree the freedom of his conscious and rational behaviour. He may not formulate a moral judgement, which, in any case, would be out of place, under pain of destroying in principle the very special type of therapeutic

[1] He can, however, and must make up his mind whether the person is sufficiently well-disposed to receive sacramental absolution.

relationship which has been established, nor should he give any advice regarding behaviour. Otherwise he will, with his subjective interference, enter into his patient's unconscious emotional conflicts and reactivate them in themselves, thus preventing him from emerging from them, from bringing them into consciousness and liquidating them, according to the technical expression. His role is limited to bringing his patient face to face with his own dynamic truth, with an approach often referred to as one of benevolent neutrality, an expression which describes it quite satisfactorily. The relationship which is established between the psychoanalyst and his patient is obviously a completely human relationship, in the sense that the therapist carries as far as it can be carried the attitude of accepting and welcoming the personality of his patient just as it is, in all its complexity; but its effective modality is placed at the infra-human level of this personality. It is quite clear that the dialogue does not take place in the world of conscious and rational relationship; it is this which constitutes the specific difference between the psycho-analytic session and any ordinary sort of conversation. It is even more clear that this dialogue cannot take place at the level of supernatural relationship. To pass a value judgement on his patient's behaviour, and even more to express such a judgement, would result in breaking the therapeutic relationship. At the very most the doctor could point out to his patient that he is deceiving himself without realizing it with regard to such and such value, on the evidence of his own words, that he is contradicting himself without noticing it, and that it would be to his advantage to find out why. For example, let us take the case of a man who affirms his belief in Christianity and his acceptance of Christian values, but is obsessed by sexual guilt: the psychoanalyst might be led to put the patient's finger on the fact that he feels things in a way which is inconsistent with the hierarchy of values he says he accepts on the rational level. According to the Christian view of values, indeed, the importance of charity is seen to be fundamental and chastity only secondary, a part of temperance, as St Thomas says. Without passing the slightest moral judgement on his patient's concrete behaviour, the psychoanalyst might be led to bring him to an awareness of the phobic hypertrophy of his sexual problems which is affecting his rational judgement.

Besides, there is no confession of sins in the analytic relationship: the patient does not have to answer to the psychoanalyst for his actions, nor to some superior entity represented by him. Now the instinctive tendency of the patient, who is always more or less charged with a neurotic feeling of guilt, is in fact to put himself in a state of anxiety about being judged. What he says often takes the form of a confession, but without his realizing it and on a level which is not that of the objectively moral order. Both with regard to method and with regard to his own attitude the psychoanalyst should take care not to enter into this unconscious game; he should consistently refuse to accept the role of judge, and should draw the patient's attention to the inadequacy of his reactions; it is obviously the only way to liquidate this primitive pseudo-moral anxiety, which very often prevents the patient making a clear judgement and freely committing himself, in accordance with a truly objective morality of relationship. By methodically refraining from making any value judgement, even an unformulated one, the psychoanalyst obliges his patient, so to speak, to 'demoralize' that which is not yet moral. It is obvious that this is a necessary preamble if the patient is to start living in accordance with a truly conscious and human sense of values, and with his own free will to assume responsibility for his own instinctive powers, as Freud's daughter, Anna Freud, says in substance in *The Ego and the Mechanisms of Defence*. It can never be sufficiently repeated that psychoanalysis is a therapy, that is to say a medical activity. Although physical comparison is always inadequate it may be said that the patient undergoing treatment does not 'confess' his unconscious to the therapist any more than the patient taken ill with acute appendicitis 'confesses' his intestines to the surgeon who operates on him.

It is usual to say that the psychoanalyst's attitude is, and ought to be, in a certain sense, frustrating. That is to say, unlike what takes place in other kinds of therapy, the psycho-analyst gives nothing. Not that his attitude ought to be one of strict coldness. But he should not enter into vibration, if one may say so, with his patient's emotional needs, which are of an archaic and regressive nature. His role is to do precisely the opposite, that is to help his patient to recognize them for what they are and to disengage himself from them. He should, therefore, refrain from responding to them, and should point them out to his patient, or help him to become aware of them. The whole psychoanalytic relationship aims at leading the patient towards an attitude of responsibility, and he must not be allowed to revert to that childish dependence to which, without realizing it, he is being imperiously drawn. That is why the treatment should not be given without payment, as that would be in contradiction with its own principle. For this reason also it must involve the patient in substantial effort, otherwise it will be indefinitely prolonged as a pleasur-able reversion to narcissism. And finally this is also why, speaking generally, and in theory, the psychoanalyst gives nothing, not even advice. When the patient asks him some-thing the analyst either does not reply or, if the stage the treatment has reached warrants it, explains to him why he has asked that question, and what need is indicated by it. Whichever he does he is limiting himself to sending the patient back to his own truth, without ever responding to his appeals.

This is a relationship, it may be seen, essentially different from the usual medical relationship, in which the patient describes the situation and receives in exchange a prescrip-tion or a precise instruction which he may unconsciously treat as a sort of magic gift. Who can ever assess the part played by instinctive psychological reactions in the efficacity of any particular medicament, already known to be efficacious on the pharmacological level?

But this relationship is even further removed from that with the confessor, which takes place at the level of supernatural healing, with all that this term may convey in a purely analogical way. In the relationship between confessor and penitent, the latter describes the situation, expresses his sorrow and his hope and receives an absolutely transcendent reality, a reality, to be sure, which he asks for with all his being, but before which he cannot be other than fundamentally receptive, since this reality, which is grace, is by definition given absolutely freely.

With the psychoanalyst the patient comes up against a refusal to accede to those regressive desires which, speaking schematically, are at the root of his neurosis. From the analytic treatment he only receives, in principle, interpretive elements which enable him to understand and to himself accept or reject those very things which up to this moment have been unconsciously conditioning his reactions and his behaviour. With the confessor, nameless instrument of an infinite gift, the penitent is all conscious receptivity before a living reality which transcends all explanation.

The difference in the setting, if one may use such an expression, indicates equally clearly the fundamental difference between these two kinds of relationship, confession and psychoanalysis. It is too often forgotten that confession, that is to say the reception of the sacrament of penance, is a liturgical act, in the most exact and strongest sense of this term. In principle, and if it is to be carried out properly, this act ought to be clothed in the same sacred solemnity as baptism or the Eucharist. The dramatic sequence, the kneeling down, the gesture and words of absolution, all this expresses, and at the same time makes real, the encounter and deepening of the intimacy between God and the sinner. Confession, wholly directed to the eternal destiny of the person receiving the sacrament, may be defined as a liturgy of progress.

Psychoanalysis, on the contrary, constitutes a situation of regression. The patient is lying down, that is to say, he is in a position of childish dependence which may also make him feel uncomfortable. The psychoanalyst is seated behind him, wrapped in this attentive neutrality about which we have just been speaking. This particular and distinctive setting is intended to facilitate the principal phase of the treatment, that is to say the transference.

By this very particular situation the patient is brought in a certain manner to relive his own unconscious and archaic conflicts in an emotional 'dialogue' with the therapist, who represents symbolically, one by one, the people in the patient's childhood who were the occasion of the unresolved conflicts. This way of presenting things is of course an over simplification but it does more or less correspond to the essential process in a form of treatment which is of necessity very complex, which varies from case to case, permits of many shades of emphasis and is very fluid. It is precisely the analysis of this transference which will enable the subject to disengage himself from his nervous tensions, since the therapist does not join in the game but consistently brings him face to face with his own reactions. This psychological phenomenon, an essential part of the psychoanalytic treatment, obviously has no place in the confessor-penitent relationship. It only intervenes at the risk of falsifying that relationship. But it is obvious, on the other hand, that if the therapist is to carry out his own duties, if he is to bring about the transference and help the subject to analyse it, he must above all take care to refrain from making any judgement in the moral order and to remain in a neutrality which is a true neutrality in this field, emotionally as well as intellectually. An excellent article by Karl Stern entitled 'psychothérapie et valeurs spirituelles' in the December 1956 issue of *La Table Ronde* brings out very well the importance of this essential neutra-

lity and of the need to avoid confusion between the psychotherapeutic technique and confession: 'It often happens', he
writes, 'in present day therapeutic experience, that a patient
produces fantastic and horrible accounts of immoral behaviour, and it is quickly seen that he would like to be blamed
for it. He wants to provoke the doctor, and expects something
in the way of a rebuke. The more certainly this desire is
frustrated, the greater is the chance of a successful transference. At the same time a particular problem of the counter-
transference arises. So long as the therapist deep within himself maintains the attitude: "Oh God, I give thee thanks that
thou hast not made me like one of these", or even a vestige of
this attitude without verbal expression, the technique will not
work.'

It often happens, in current practice, that a Catholic who is
mentally ill will need both these situations between which
we have tried to draw such a sharp distinction. That is to
say that he will have to go alternately to the psychoanalyst
and the confessor. From this problems will arise and it is
essential that each of these two keeps strictly to his own field,
despite the attempt that patients often make, naturally without realizing it, to bring about confusion. Even if the psychoanalyst, well trained by his own teaching analysis, takes care
to avoid confusion, in accordance with what Karl Stern
writes, it may happen that the confessor, with the best of
intentions but with little knowledge of the realities of depth
psychology, will allow himself, for his part, to be drawn by
his patient into making reactions or observations that will in
fact interfere with the analytic relationship.

This brings us straight away to another distinction that
should be made, a distinction which seems too often to be
passed over in silence in the current of present-day thought:
the difference between the role of the priest as minister of
the sacrament of penance and the role of what is known as a
spiritual director (*directeur de conscience*).

The first is essentially an instrumental role. The priest acts as a priest, that is to say as charged with a supernatural power infinitely beyond him, as directly delegated by Christ and the Church to dispense the mystery of mercy. In principle his own psychological and spiritual personality does not enter as a constituent element into the relationship between the penitent and the mystery of the living God which is established in the course of the liturgical situation of the sacrament. In principle the minister's own personality should not play any greater part than in the eucharistic or baptismal liturgy. The minister of the sacrament, strictly as minister, is anonymous; and one can easily think of a confession reduced to its essential elements—confession of sins, religious, but not moral, admonition, and the words of absolution.

The relationship which is established between the subject and the spiritual director is quite different. It is not, in itself, in any way sacramental; and by contrast the personality of the director enters fully into it. There is always some risk involved because it is liable to give rise to the most complex psychological reactions, conscious and otherwise. The very term spiritual director (*directeur de conscience*) is ambiguous. It could be taken to indicate a certain idea of dependence, of passive submission, of absolute authority, all of which would tend to keep the spiritual liberty of the person concerned in leading strings and under the control of another human being. And so without either of them realizing it, there may well arise those phenomena of the transference and the counter-transference that enter to a greater or lesser degree into all human relationships, but more easily in a situation of childish dependence. If the director starts analysing the transference he is abandoning his own role for that of the therapist, for which he is not trained. But if he is unaware, or wishes to be unaware, of the reality of these psychological reactions, he may allow himself to be drawn into giving advice or taking up positions which can be quite harmful. The expressions 'spiritual adviser' and 'spiritual father' are perhaps less ambiguous. The first carries with it more the idea of respect for the liberty of the subject. The second calls up the idea of generation and stresses that the role of the spiritual father is to bring the subject to the spiritual life, that is to say, to help him become adult and free in this direction as in the direction of natural life. It is only too easily forgotten that the role of the spiritual director is precisely to teach the person who consults him how to direct himself. The spiritual life cannot be a satisfactory personal relationship with God if there is continually present an intermediary who interposes the barrier of his own authority.

This is quite apart from the possibility of this authority being understood in a dictatorial sense, as paternalist rather than paternal, which by this very fact would engage the whole complex affectivity of the director, an affectivity which may be neurotic.

Spiritual advice as such engages neither the sacramental power nor the sacramental character of the adviser or 'father'. It is not, of itself, a priestly function. This is proved by the fact that in congregations of religious who are not priests it is exercised by superiors and novice masters who have not received holy orders, and this applies also to congregations of religious sisters. The relationship which is established in the sacrament of penance issues in a supernatural and mysterious result which is, if one may say so, infinitely absolute, but the result of the dialogue which is established in the giving and receiving of spiritual advice remains essentially relative, in the sense that the two people involved are no more than two human people, with all their frailties and the possibility of mistakes on both sides. And it is absolutely necessary that this fundamental distinction should be clearly present in the mind of both of them if the relationship is to be fruitful and not act as a barrier to the mysterious action of grace, or to the freedom of the person asking advice. Nothing is more harmful, as much from the religious point of view as the psychological, than a director who demands blind and absolute obedience; it is very likely that, without realizing it, he is satisfying a more or less suspect and selfish need to dominate which has nothing to do with his role as director.

If account is taken of this essential difference it will be seen that there is far more risk of interference between the psychoanalyst and the spiritual father than there is between the psychoanalyst and the confessor, the nameless minister of the sacrament as such. If the greatest possible respect is paid to confession as being religious, liturgical and mystical in the ontological sense of this term, the penitent who is mentally ill will be officially placed in a situation which is the very opposite of that of psychoanalysis, and this will help him to get out of that confusion which he often, without knowing it, is trying to perpetuate.

But the spiritual adviser of a patient being analysed should be particularly careful not to fall into the temptation of paternalism, a term which a certain fairly recent usage, and perhaps also a certain faulty emphasis in doctrine, makes particularly suggestive. In a very general sense it may be said in effect that a neurotic person suffers from a fixation to the emotional attitudes of his childhood past. That is to say, he has not arrived at a positive psychological liberty in his capacity for making relationships. Without realizing it he instinctively puts himself in a situation of greater dependence than other people, or in a situation which calls for greater dependence. In order to reach psychological and spiritual maturity he has a greater need than other people have for this emotional need not to be answered, so that he is tacitly obliged to assume responsibility for his own decisions and consequent risks. While the psychoanalyst confronts him with the hidden springs of his own behaviour, the spiritual adviser should encourage him as much as he can to achieve that freedom and capacity to make decisions on his own which is necessary if the spiritual life is to be a truly personal response to the mystery of the divine call and the divine love. One cannot be truly a child before God unless one has sufficiently grown out of childish reactions before men. And the neurotic tends in one way or another to turn every situation into a childish one. This tendency expresses itself most often in all its strength in the dialogue with his 'spiritual father'. It is obviously desirable that the spiritual father should not allow himself to be caught, and should often refuse to give positive advice which, psychologically speaking, would amount to acting in the place of the subject, and preventing him from being himself. This will sometimes require real courage and even the appearance of cruelty on the part of the spiritual adviser: it is sometimes very hard to have to leave a mentally ill person to the anxiety of having to make a decision for which he is not yet able to take responsibility. But to make the decision for him would be to do him serious harm; it is a temptation to take the easy way out and to a false charity which would obstruct the work of liberation and of development which is being carried out in the analysis.

Again, the mentally ill person who is obsessed by religious problems always tends to a greater or lesser degree to 'psychologize' the supernatural and the spiritual life. That is, to a greater or lesser degree, he confuses the emotional sphere and the sphere of faith, always without clearly realizing it. His relationship with God is often affected by emotional elements which persist in his childish relationship with the adult world, and especially with his parents. God will often be envisaged as a 'super-father'; Our Lady, or the Church, will be envisaged as a 'super-mother'. It is necessary for the spiritual adviser to help the subject to distinguish the purely psychological field more and more clearly from the field which is really spiritual. What is necessary is that the person should be gradually brought to realize the real transcendence of the divine mystery, in himself as well as in his relationship with us. That the subject should disengage his knowledge of God as he has revealed himself from the anthropomorphic projections which take place without his realizing it. God is not only a father: he is the mysterious unity of three Persons. Christ is not only an affectionate brother: he is the unity of human and divine life in the Person of the Word. Our Lady is not, strictly speaking, 'our heavenly mother' (*notre maman du ciel*), which is in any case a childish and ambiguous expression: she is the one person who is completely open to the presence of God, with all that that represents in the way of scriptural references, of universality, and of religious depth, going far beyond emotional reactions. This delicate work of purifying the spiritual life, which is a long and difficult matter even for those who are psychologically normal, is often particularly so for neurotics. It is here that the spiritual adviser needs all his patience and all his most authentic religious sense in order not to condone or aggravate a confusion which is always harmful.

As Dr Hesnard has brought out very well, neurosis is often linked in one way or another with a false feeling of guilt, which is nothing but an unconscious pathological anxiety, having little relation to the religious meaning of penance. In this case the practice of confession can give rise to problems. Certain mentally ill persons suffering from scruples feel a need for confession which is really neurotic, confession being for them nothing but a sort of magic exorcism of their anxiety. Apart from the fact that this necessarily devalues the sacramental mystery, it can condone the neurosis, or even make it worse if the confessor acts more as a 'moralist' than as a minister of this mystery.

An example will make this clear. Mme F., aged about 40, suffers from an obsessional neurosis. Among other symptoms she experiences a truly overwhelming and compulsional fear of 'mortal sin' on the least occasion—the way in which she gets into a train on the underground, drinking a cup of coffee, Friday abstinence, etc. She feels a compelling need to go to confession, five or six times a week, and sometimes more. In order to bring her to a more healthy spiritual life it is clear that, while the psychoanalyst is helping her to become aware of the unconscious source of her troubles, the spiritual adviser should discourage such frequent confession: he should refuse to take part in this obsessional game, should rule out of the confession of sins all those which appear to be related to the obsession and tirelessly insist on the religious character of the sacrament in the framework of faith in salvation through Christ. That is, the confessor will be led to 'demoralize' confession as far as he possibly can in order to make it an occasion for a theological instruction on hope.

Caught between the psychoanalyst who confronts him with the truth on a psychological level, and the confessor who refuses to enter into the unconscious game of pseudo-religious or pseudo-moral rationalization, the mentally ill person will be summoned, so to speak, often at the cost of a very hard trial, to purify his spiritual attitude of all that is tainting it, so that he can at the same time reach psychological equilibrium and an authentic relationship with God.

Those who try to bring pastoral and modern psychology together so that each may be enriched by learning something from the other are sometimes reproached with no longer believing in the efficacity of the supernatural. But this reproach is ill-founded: to distinguish the supernatural as clearly as possible from natural means is not to deny it, but is rather the contrary. The sacramental mystery is not intended in itself to be a psychotherapy and its efficacity is therefore essentially in the supernatural order.

On the other hand, in this existential zone of pastoral activity, which borders at the same time on the psychological life and on the mystery of faith, ignorance of clinical psychology may represent a real danger. It happens only too often that a well-intentioned confessor condones a neurotic obsession by allowing a penitent to make an unwise use of the sacrament, or at least that he does not consider the psychopathological aspect of the problem, thinking that prayer and sacramental grace will solve everything. One still sometimes hears it said: 'Psychotherapy? I don't believe in it.' As if one

could, *mutatis mutandis*, 'believe in' penicillin or appendic-
ectomy! In this way a mentally ill person can continue to
take refuge in an obsessional anxiety of a sexual nature, for
which he has an unconscious need, in order, in fact, not to
have to come out of himself. His confessions, far from being
therapeutic, are used by him, with the best will in the world,
as a more or less masochistic return to the situations of conflict which do not wish to be resolved. They have nothing to
do with the sacrament itself, any more than with the life of
relationship with God, despite the appearances and the expressions used.

Another aspect of this lack of knowledge should be emphasized, all the more briefly for the fact that the practice of
analytic psychotherapy is fortunately spreading in medical
practice today. It should be understood that a psychoanalyst
of integrity and competence never gives positive advice. One
hears it said fairly often that a patient undergoing psychoanalysis has received from his doctor the advice, for example,
to get divorced or to take a mistress. If the psychoanalyst in
question is properly qualified this will be false, without any
manner of doubt, because such a practice would be the very
negation of the analytic method. But it may well happen that
the patient, at a certain stage of his treatment, discovers
disordered or chaotic impulses in himself, impulses that he
cannot as yet freely take responsibility for and keep in their
right place; he may then, completely in good faith, attribute
to his analyst ideas which are only in himself, but which he
is unable as yet to recognize as his own and to re-orientate.

It sometimes happens, and this perhaps more frequently,
that the mentally ill person tries unconsciously to make use of
his spiritual adviser to break off the treatment, when this is
reaching a stage he is unwilling to enter. This resistance
manoeuvre consists in going to his confessor and telling him
that the psychoanalyst is giving him bad advice: this is not
true, but the patient is sincere in interpreting things in such a
way that the confessor can say to him in the name of moral

authority: 'Stop the analysis!' It is therefore necessary, in order to avoid entering into his game, to know that the patient without realizing it is basically distorting things. The psychoanalyst limits himself to pointing out to his patient that he is, for example, experiencing an ambivalent aggressiveness towards his wife, who to a certain extent represents his mother for his unconscious; but he never advises him to do such and such. The confessor should know this, so that he can help to right the situation, and help the penitent who is mentally ill to face up to his own responsibilities.

If it can be dangerous for a confessor or a spiritual adviser to be unaware of psychological realities, it can be equally dangerous for a confessor to try his hand at psychotherapy. This amounts to not respecting the difference between the two orders. A series of spiritual talks with an adviser well-informed psychologically can often be beneficial, it is true, but only if the adviser takes account of what he has been able to understand of his visitor's problems in order to help him with his spiritual life, without entering into the study or the clarification of those problems in themselves. If he does happen to have the competence, and decides to tackle these problems, it should be with full knowledge of what he is doing, on his side as well as on the side of the penitent; that is to say, the relationship which is established will become a psychotherapeutic relationship, and no longer a specifically priestly one. So much so that it is preferable for the adviser to send the person to another priest, and to make every attempt in his own attitude to keep the psychological field quite separate from that sacramental field which he is taking care not to enter.

The psychoanalytic relationship is in a certain sense an infra-human one; that is to say, the transference phenomenon makes the therapy a sort of support for the reliving and liquidation of emotional situations which are regressive and archaic. The relationship involved in spiritual advice, and even more, that of the sacrament of penance, is orientated in the opposite direction, to the supra-human; that is to say, the minister of the mystery is simply an instrument for the personal discovery of God, which is the exact opposite of chaos and regression. It would be exceedingly harmful, and on some occasions even catastrophic, to mix these two relationships: if they are experienced by one subject with the same person they can only cancel each other out: the spiritual relationship always suffers, but the confusion which is engendered also prevents the transference from being beneficial, and the neurotic situation only entrenches itself the more firmly.

For this reason, among others, a psychoanalyst habitually refuses to see a patient's spiritual director except in his presence. It is necessary that everything should be clear, and that the patient, to the extent of his potential receptivity, should be faced with his own psychological truth and with transcendent truth, without his being able to mix the two, and play about with one in order to obscure the other.

The psychoanalyst's place is at the point of the confused origins of his patient's emotional life, which he tries to clarify from below, if one may put it that way, so that the patient may come to know himself, orientate himself and build himself up again more freely.

The confessor's place is at the point of the meeting between the person of his penitent and that of Christ his Saviour, and he is the instrument of a quite different illumination, from above, to use an expression dear to Pseudo-Dionysius.

Both for the sake of objective truth and for the sake of the human and spiritual aspects of any neurosis, whether serious or not, it is essential not to confuse these two roles and to know well that, if they should both be necessary at the same time, in no case can either of them replace the other.

FREUD, RELIGION AND CIVILIZATION

Louis Beirnaert

It is usual to present Freud as an opponent of Christianity, and to regard psychoanalysis as being for this reason radically perverted. One remark must be made at the ouset—the religion rejected by Freud is not the religion revealed to us by the Holy Scriptures and the teaching of the Church. It can be shown by reference to the text how the authentic Judeo-Christian doctrine has been transformed in the account, or rather reconstruction, of it which Freud gives. One example will suffice. In several places Freud states that in Christianity the Son takes the place of the Father. This regardless of the clearest articles of faith. Freud's rejection, then, is the rejection of a religion which has been distorted, but the distortion is his own work.

Another thing is equally important. It is said and written fairly generally that Freud would have substituted the worship of science for the worship of God. It is in vain that one looks for any such value judgement in the work of this thinker who was always calling attention to our lack of certainty and to the very small extent to which human behaviour is influenced by science, but quite apart from this it seems clear that if Freud has put anything in the place of God it is not science, but death. His whole view of man's life in society implies that it is inexorably dominated by the fear of a death which weighs upon all of those who would set out to realize their unlimited desire for existence. Civilized man, according to Freud, is a slave whose master is death.

This is of interest for a true understanding of psychoanalysis. It is not, in fact, in opposition to religion as such, but in opposition to civilization, with its prohibitions imposed under pain of death, that psychoanalysis sets out to restore the individual desire for self-assertion and also love, in so far as it is based upon the fundamental relationship of man with woman and woman with man, for mutual joy and procreation. Against the background of the domination of human life by death, psychoanalysis appears as the restoration of something fundamental, that is sexual love, not only in itself, but in its character of 'prototype of all happiness', in its *Vorbildichkeit*.

Freud attributed the cause of neurosis ultimately to civilization and regarded religion, on the contrary, as protecting people from individual neurosis. For all that he does not accept religion, because, according to the picture of it which he paints for himself, it is founded on the imaginary restoration of the parental figures of childhood. Religion only protects the individual by making him take part in a collective illusion, socializing, certainly, but now in the sphere of the unreal. Because, whatever he may write about the constraint placed by death upon the history of humanity, it is death that he accepts. There is nothing for him to do except bow his head before Ananke, hard though her law may be. To hold any belief which shows history as dominated by a benevolent power which would lead men to happiness is to resort to an illusion, an imaginary extension into historical proportions of that which happens to us all when we are little children.

In this way Freud set up an antithesis between a religious belief in a benevolent father, and a realistic submission to the domination of death. In order to understand how this opposition developed in Freud's mind it is necessary to go back to his account of the common origin of civilization and religion: the primordial crime, the murder of the primal father.

This myth opens up an essential aspect of Freud's thought.

As soon as the all-powerful father who possessed all the women came to represent for the brothers of the primal horde the realization of their desire, the father, stronger than they, drove them away and barred them from happiness. They wanted to be everything and to have everything, like him. But they could not satisfy their desires except by risking their lives in a relentless struggle. They were defeated, or rather they were driven away without any struggle taking place. It is interesting to see here how Freud, without realizing it, refashioned the Hegelian dialectic of master and slave. The father, this pre-human creature moved only by his desires, did not fight and defeat his sons and reduce them to slavery, attaching them to himself, but instead he drove them to a distance. The sons in their turn, instead of experiencing what it was to be robbed of the fruits of their enforced labour, and so discovering their power over the nature they cultivated, themselves remain pre-human and moved only by desire. Nothing can be expected from the exile which they experience together except a recognition of their common exclusion—of their quality of being 'equally persecuted by the father'.

So, the recognition of the slave by the master who takes for himself the fruit of the slave's labour, and of the master by the slave who has been allowed his life, is replaced by a purely horizontal recognition in terms of another person whose power so far as the sons is concerned is purely negative. The difference is due to the fact that in the Freudian dialectic between the father of the horde and his sons the object of enjoyment is not just a natural object which it is possible to make the slave produce, but the sexual object which is already given, and with regard to which there is no alternative but to keep away anyone who wishes to lay hand on it. Slave labour is of no use to the master here.

But the situation in which they find themselves, of being equally excluded from the sexual enjoyment of the women, because it constitutes for them a situation of privation under constraint, brings about a transformation of the sons' sexual nature. They identify themselves one with the other and, according to Freud, bind themselves together with homosexual ties, with the result that that which in the father leads to separation in them leads to universalization. Then, becoming aware of the powerfulness of being united, they are able to do together what would have been impossible for each of them alone—kill the father.

In doing this they are in fact killing an animal which has continued to be led exclusively by the desire for immediate enjoyment and the wild jealousy of a possessive male. Freud cannot find words enough to describe the brutality and unlimited narcissism of the father of the horde. It is equally significant that he had to pass through totemism in order to bring the father into his idea of social origins. Nevertheless at this stage of their consciousness, this father is the sons' ideal, their *Vorbild*. And so they bring about their identification with him in the same way as they would with a dead animal —by eating him.

The father is dead; from now on they wish, one and all, to be the father and take his place. Was it not precisely in order to satisfy their desire to be everything, and to possess all the women, like him, that they killed him? But now something new has come into their consciousness—the vision of death, wating for whoever becomes like the father. And so, for the mutual protection of their lives and to safeguard each one from the possibility of the lot which befell the father, they forbid themselves the fruits of their action, renouncing the use of the father's wives, and prohibiting murderous aggression. From now on nobody will be father. The whole of civilization has as its aim to prevent this inextinguishable desire from ever being realized by anybody. And so direct sexual tendencies are inhibited and transformed into gentle feelings to check the aggressive instinct, and the aggressive instinct itself is turned back into agression against oneself and into guilt.

Let us stop here. Freud's thought is clear; it only remains

to interpret it. What is the significance for civilized man of the situation in which he finds himself when there is no longer any father?

It is not basically so very different from the situation of the sons in the primal horde suffering equal persecution. The repression of instinct operates on all sides with humanizing results. On all sides this situation is maintained by violence: the violence of one against all in the pre-historic horde: the violence of all against one in the history of human society. In a letter to Einstein on the problem of war Freud wrote: 'Violence could be broken by union, and the power of those who were united now represented law in contrast to the violence of the single individual... Right is the might of a community. It is still violence, ready to be directed against any individual who resists it: it works by the same methods and follows the same purposes.'[1] If the force exercised by a community takes on the character of law it is because men recognize that it makes possible life in common, or more precisely perhaps, survival in common. The co-operation of everyone is required to keep the father out.

The father, however, is always being re-established figuratively by the desire inherent in each man to satisfy his will to power and by his desire for exclusive possession. The father is as powerful dead as alive. Each one aspires to take his place: is he not the *Vorbild*, the envied model? But at the same time everyone is led to kill him continually in everybody else because his actual re-establishment would mean death.

It follows that as soon as men have disencumbered themselves of the one father, they then spend their time protecting themselves from the potential master which each one of us represents for all the others. Their liberation is condemned to remain purely formal, because at the very moment it is on the point of being actualized, it is immediately checked by the fear of death. And so the movement is continually

[1] 'Why War?', *Collected Papers*, V, p. 275.

repeated: all together killing the father in each one, to maintain the ideal liberty which was achieved by the murder
committed once in reality, and to preserve life here and now.

And from this also in a sort of acceptance of fate, of this
destiny in which Freud could recognize the face of the terrible father, 'Auch das Schicksal ist nur ein späterer Vater-
projektion',[1] there follows the murder of the father in oneself:
the eventual identification of oneself with the dead father.
And so death for the civilized person, according to Freud,
is at the same time both feared and desired; it is the real
Vorbild as opposed to the imaginary *Vorbild*. Freud has a
religion of death.

And from here it can be shown how Freud, when treating
of the last things, makes death actually play the role of the
father. Death was present at the beginnings of life, 'the non-
living precedes the living', and is its goal: 'death is the goal
towards which tends all life.' Death is the ultimate authority
and leads man towards its own likeness, and thence to liberation in the truth. It begets humanity out of itself in a movement which is never anything but a return to the previous
state. It is death which brings about the real identification
with the father.

This is a hard thought, terrible for man's will to existence,
but Freud did not think the desires of man could be satisfied.
His whole critique of religion shows this very clearly. As we
go into it further we shall see swing open in front of us the
other panel of the Freudian diptych of views about the world.

Religion has the same origin as civilization. But it is derived
from another source. Once the murder has been carried out
and the aggression put into action, love of the father arises
again in the brothers in the form of remorse. Their longing
for the father (*Vatersehnsucht*) and their desire to disavow their
action leads them to re-establish the father figuratively in
forms which finally culminate in the one God of the Judeo-

[1] 'Dostoevsky and Parricide', *Collected Papers*, V, p. 222.

Christian religion. By a 'retrospective obedience' they now submit themselves to the will which they have offended, on the assumption that the father will on this account continue to dispense the protection and the benefits which he formerly assured them. By all manner of practices and rites they seek reconciliation with the father. It is in the Christian teaching, particularly as presented by St Paul, that the meaning of religion is expressed most clearly: the offence to the father is recognized and reconciliation is brought about by the sacrifice of one in the name of all.

This, Freud says, is a reaction formation which can never be successful, because it is founded on an ambivalent attitude towards the father, who is at the same time hated and loved, and can never resolve this ambivalence: in the Christian version the ambivalence goes so far as to find expression in the replacement of the Father by the Son. It is also an illusion in as much as it ignores reality, which necessarily frustrates men's desires, and substitutes for it a Providence charged with assuring their satisfaction, just as the parents in early childhood saw to the needs of the defenceless child.

This brief summary of the Freudian view of the origin of religion is sufficient as a basis for reflection.

The question is, where does the love for the father come from? The description Freud has given us of the primal father affords absolutely no ground for it. In so far as the murder is explained by bitter rivalry between oppressor and oppressed it is incomprehensible that it should be regretted. Freud himself is surprised that man can feel guilty of 'a crime of which he should be so proud.' The father of human prehistory, as described by Freud, has nothing lovable about him. This is a very strong indication that the origin of what we have here is still to be sought. If the father of the horde with his unlimited narcissism provides insufficient grounds for the love which is entertained for him it follows that the father whose death is regretted must be another father. The idea of him is derived from another source than that of the horde father.

Where, then, could man have got the idea of a father who is at the same time loved and feared, whom one obeys and whose favour one wishes to gain, except from the family itself? Freud is describing a father who accepts his sons as his own, and who is accepted by the sons as their father.

Such a father certainly imposes a law on the child; he rewards and punishes. But he is benevolent, bringing his children up and dispensing benefits to them, and he loves them. Freud recognizes this paternal love. 'The indestructible strength of the family as a natural group formation,' he writes, 'rests upon the fact that this necessary presupposition of the father's equal love can have a real application in the family.'[1] It is only on the basis of some such empirical evidence that any sort of love for the father on the part of the sons is conceivable. The horde father, then, is not the whole father.

Just as remarkable is the fact that Freud regards the extension of the son-father relationship, originating in the family, to the social group, as an 'idealistic remodelling of the state of affairs in the primal horde, where all the sons knew that they were equally *persecuted* by the primal father, and feared him equally.'[2] It is in the Jewish religion that Freud sees this. He says it was due to the sons failing to accept their position of independence as adult men, henceforward without support, after the crime which liberated them; instead they let their thoughts go back to earlier days, and re-established, figuratively, the father of times past. By so doing they avoided the necessity of recognizing the mastery of death.

Here, then, we have two opposing solutions of the problem put to man by his will to existence. He can either accept the domination of death and submit to the law which inhibits his instinctive desires; or he can deny this domination, and re-establish the figure of a benevolent father who will see to

[1] *Group Psychology and the Analysis of the Ego*, Standard Ed., Vol. XVIII, p. 125.
[2] *Ibid.*, p. 124.

the satisfaction of these same desires. This second solution is
an imaginary one; we think that the first is just as imaginary,
although in another sense. But we think, above all, with Freud
himself, that neither one nor the other is a sufficient basis
for civilization.[1]

The religious solution as presented by Freud shows, at the
very least, that the death of another person has resolved
nothing. It witnesses, in its own way, not only to the futility,
but even to the harmfulness, of the crime. The very fact that
Freud talks about a universal neurosis shows well enough
that there is an underlying problem still unresolved, a conflict which is always present: that between love and hate.
Indeed, wherever the other person appears always as the
strong, claiming sovereignty and exclusive use for himself,
the son remaining a slave, revolt alternates with love. And
this really was the case under the Jewish law. 'Now I say,
as long as the heir is a child, he differeth nothing from a slave,
though he be lord of all; but he is under tutors and governors
until the time appointed by the father: so we also, when we
were children, were in bondage to the elements of the world.
But when the fulness of the time was come, God sent his Son,
made of a woman...'[2] The difference between St Paul and
Freud is that the former considers the position under the Jewish
law in relation to Christ—in the slave he sees the heir, who is
already 'lord of all', and the Father is really seen as a father
in the liberation brought about by his Son—whereas Freud
describes the position under the Jewish law in relation to death,
seeing in the son a slave who does not want to rebel, or rather
a slave who is continually trying to deny his rebellion. We
shall see that the distinction between Freud's view of religion
as a universal neurosis, and the religion of St Paul, lies just here.

[1] We should like to make it clear that we are here referring to the
religious solution as presented by Freud, and as it is perhaps accepted
in practice at a certain level by some believers, but not to the Christian
solution as it is presented by the Holy Scriptures and by the Church.

[2] Gal. 4. 1–4. (The Douay has 'servant' in place of 'slave' and 'serving
under' in place of 'in bondage to.' – Tr.)

Religion, according to Freud, is a universal neurosis, which nevertheless spares the individual from an individual neurosis. Slavery under the dominion of death is a universal truth, which nevertheless gives rise to individual neurosis. Here again the problem of being has not been resolved by the death of another person. Individual neurosis, also, witnesses to the conflict between revolt and submission which is always present in every human heart. But it is not the same thing which is overlooked in each case. If religion, putting love in the foreground, pays insufficient attention to the aggressive instincts associated with the ego, civilization for its part pays insufficient attention to sexuality and the instincts of life. It is probable that a careful study of the significance of these opposing tendencies, point by point, and of the complementary nature of these conflicts would throw some light on the deeper meaning of Freud's work. We shall content ourselves with pointing out the problems, dialectically linked together, towards which, on Freud's own admission, the childish religious solution and submission to the categorical imperatives of a civilization dominated by death both converge.

And so psychoanalysis, as we said at the beginning, may well be regarded as a work of rediscovery. By setting itself to re-establish in the subject his capacity for sexual love, it snatches from the dominion of death something which is essential, not only to the life and happiness of the individual, but also to the existence of human society, for which the relationship of love between man and wife, father, mother and children, serves as a model.

The question then arises, why Freud did not finish the movement which he helped to inaugurate? One may answer, because he could not carry it to its conclusion so long as he remained dominated by his view of civilization. Man is divided, in this view, between the search for individual happiness in love and family life, and the imperatives of a civilization which maintains itself by the repression of the sexual instincts. He is not one. Worse, he has no principle of unity; that is to say, there is no sign of anything in him which could pass beyond the opposition between the terms of the anti- nomy and begin to build up a constructive synthesis. And so the conflict which should enable the new man to be born is forced down to the biological or even quantitative level and becomes a problem of 'the economy of the individual libido', of a suitable distribution of the 'libidinal energy' between the pursuit of the direct ends of sexual love and submission to the constraints of civilization. In looking for a solution to the problem of distribution Freud oscillates between an appeal to biology and bodily constitution, and an appeal to the essential mystery of the subject, so far as it dominates the terms of the antinomy.

What is the cause of this flaw in Freud's reasoning? Of the separation he finally maintains between the movement of the 'love which is the foundation of the family' and the movement of aggression which is the foundation of human society, through the master-slave relation resulting from a fight to the death? Freud thinks that the only group which can bring about the interaction of these two movements is the family. In the family the love of the marriage partners, who go on to procreate children, forms the basis of a reciprocal recogni- tion of the husband by the wife and of the children by their parents. A recognition which permeates more and more deeply the relation of master and slave which maintains the dominion of husband over wife and of parents over children, while, conversely, the dominion of master over slave gradually detaches love from the pursuit of immediate satisfaction, and progressively directs it towards the pursuit of values which can be made universal.[1]

But Freud does not think that what takes place in the heart of the family, and continually renews itself there, can become at the same time universal and real with regard to the com-

[1] Cf. G. Fessard, 'Le mystère de la Société,' *Recherche de Science reli- gieuse*, January and April 1948.

munity. The frontier barrier between family and society is closed. The whole of love in its positive function of promoting existence for everyone remains on the one side, and the whole of aggressiveness, so far as it gives rise to universalizing relationship under the aegis of death, remains on the other. So that, considered in relation to the family from which he comes, and the one he is going to found, a man reaches fulfilment, but considered in relation to the wider society in which he takes his place as an equal member, he remains a slave, to death, to the law and to guilt; and with no escape.

If only Freud had pushed to its limit the interaction between the recognition of love founded on creative sexuality on the one hand, and the master-slave relationship founded on the struggle to death between individuals on the other, he would have reached the point where the master himself renounces his will to power out of love, 'non rapinam arbitratus est esse se æqualem Deo', and freely makes himself a slave, 'exinanivit semetipsum, formam servi accipiens', and freely submits himself to death, 'factus obediens usque ad mortem', showing death not as the universal lord, but as vanquished, despoiled of his power: 'et mors ultra non dominabitur'. St Paul's teaching resolves Freud's problems. The Jew become Christian answers the unbelieving Jew and delivers him from his chains.

With Freud's unbelief and his Judaism we come to the central point of his position. It can be shown that he regressed to the stage of giving a Greek solution to a problem which could only be set by a man brought up on the Bible—as he was, on his own admission—and by a member of a Jewish minority in the middle of a Christian world. By whom, ultimately, are the brothers equally presecuted, if not by the solid Christian majority that the young Freud came up against in his childhood and youth, particularly at the University of Vienna? It looks as if this always came between Freud and what he learnt about Christianity. He never managed to disengage his knowledge of Christianity from the factual conditions under which he met it. This accounts for his constant revolt, and also his submission. It was on his return from Rome in 1901 that he learnt that 'the old world is governed by authority just as the new is governed by the dollar', and that he made his bow to those who dispose of power and positions. It is necessary to live reasonably well and to get one's work done. Freud allowed himself to be deceived by the only too human face of an established religion, which at one and the same time touches on magical ways of thought and on domination by those in possession. He had no knowledge of the real Christianity and himself fell back under the dominion of death, law and guilt. A Jew, then, but an unbelieving Jew who made of his powers not teachers in the service of freedom, but slaves of a Greek Ananke.

According to Freud a psychoanalyst is someone who fights against this, so that human love may exist at least in the individual and in the family unit, so that Eros, with his tendency to unite all men, should have the victory there at least.

But the analytic 'moment' cannot be isolated and erected into an absolute without constituting a paganism. It is only out of the conflict between the rediscovered gentile and the Jew who is still a slave that the new man may be born, as the one who will reconcile these two. Because he has always kept the conflict open, Freud is not the pagan that he is often painted, but a torn and tragic man, among whose notes may be caught the echoes of the complaints of Job.

A DANGEROUS DOCTRINE

Étienne Borne

The list of objections

When Freudian doctrine talks about the unconscious, repression, the censor, the transference, sublimation, it goes beyond psychoanalytic therapy and bursts open the Freudian system, turning it into current speech and putting it into everybody's mouth. And so Freudianism is mixed in with the spirit of our civilization, and perhaps expresses one of its major anxieties. It does this by whipping up rapids and whirlpools, by contradicting and being contradicted; it does this by putting a question. It is the dialectic of this conflict that it is intended broadly to describe here, for Freudianism is a fighting doctrine and aims at a fairly radical demystification of man, its violence calling out violence in opposition; it is a provocative and aggressive doctrine, whether for better or worse, and it risks calling in question man's true balance as well as his aberrant constructions and his false and conventional stabilizations. Freudianism suffers from a fundamental ambiguity, which it is impossible to clear up completely, and which explains at the same time its power of penetration (for boldness and chiaroscuro always have a strong appeal) and the sharp opposition it cannot help but arouse. Freud is of the stature of Marx and Nietzsche, those other geniuses of demystification, like them an enemy of the established order, and like them profoundly dangerous.

There will, then, be a Christian polemic against Freud as

there is a Christian polemic against Marx and against Nietzsche, and it will be particularly strong in those traditional milieux where strictness is confused with the systematic practice of condemnation and rejection. Freud's hypotheses are in themselves intolerable to the moral and religious conscience—duty as the gradual crystallization of ancestral prohibitions and primitive taboos, stripped in consequence of any transcendental origin or import; responsibility torn to shreds by the mechanism of repression and censorship; individual existence nothing but the result of biological and sociological forces; the sacred explained by a morbid and analysable fear before a power which is in the long run social and unconscious. Will not the uniqueness of Christianity fall to pieces if faith in the God-man who sacrifices himself to save man from evil is nothing but a gigantic interpretive illusion constructed by the anxiety of guilt in a self-punishment complex known to psychoanalysis and regarded by it as closed?

The Christian polemic against Freudianism, then, will not lack strong arguments, and it will not accept the thesis that the Freudian theory, so obviously repugnant, can be separated from a beneficial and acceptable psychoanalytic technique. How can the link between cause and effect be broken, and does not psychoanalysis set in action the whole of the Freudian doctrine? Are not moral problems reduced by strict Freudian theory to psychological obstructions which can be resolved and dissolved by a competent expert in the workings of the mind? Will not the sense of sin be destroyed? Is not psychoanalytic treatment a naturalistic imitation of spiritual direction and Catholic confession, and does not the liberation it brings about consist in the promise of an original innocence to be found beyond good and evil? If such an indictment were both true and consistent it would mean that Freudian doctrine and the spirit of Christianity are engaged in a fight to the death, and that the success of psychoanalysis indicates a decline in Christian civilization.

The Marxist polemic shows itself no less intransigent

against Freudianism than the Christian. At least in the time of Stalin psychoanalysts had no citizenship rights in the communist empire and Freudian doctrine is usually rejected by Marxist propagandists as obscurantist, as a product of the breaking up of the bourgeois world, as individualism, as indulging in a purely theoretical argument, as a taste for that introspection which Politzer brusquely said was as much mythology as an imperfection of Freudian doctrine. Marxism cannot admit that man may be his own mystifier, because for Marxism all mystification comes to man from outside and is due to defects in the social organism. And so Marxism sees no universal value in the Freudian doctrine and regards it as simply a reflection of the contradictions which result from a disintegrating capitalism.

So speaks the communist inquisitor. And at the heart of the polemics which are carried on against Freudianism by Marxist and Christian 'integrity' alike may be found a similar anxiety. Once Marxism has become a fighting ideology, or more exactly, a poetry of action, it cannot admit the jurisdiction of psychoanalytic technique over the origin and genesis of its dogmas and myths; Freud is the provoker of doubt who must be driven away from the community of believers: a red Athens would not tolerate this Socrates. And if many of the Christian objections to Freudianism are justifiable both on natural and on religious grounds, it is possible all the same for a narrow and jealous Christianity to refuse to run the risk of the psychoanalytic method exposing that systematic aggressiveness which is a quite frequent corruption of dogmatic faith. In either case an inquisition of inquisitions is not regarded as fair play and provokes so absolute a refusal as to give rise to suspicion.

And finally there must be included in the list of objections that quarantine to which Freudianism has been forced to submit for so long by the rationalist and idealist doctrine which is substantially the philosophy of the French universities. Alain made the irreversible decision of paying Freud no attention whatsoever, and taught that there was nothing in the contradictory and confused idea of the unconscious but a very mediocre romanticism which, if maintained for long, would turn into a sin against reason. Alain regards man as a sovereign being who cannot be dispossessed of his free will except by his own cowardice, and so Freudianism will be kept severely at a distance because it is said to be guilty of organizing man's capitulation to shadowy forces which in any case are imaginary. Sartre's existentialism, despite his break with the rationalism of the universities, echoes Alain's harshness towards the unconscious. So much so that Sartre's conception of man, as completely illuminated by the light of a *cogito* which is being continually renewed, seems at first glance to be the exact opposite of Freud's: the very structure of consciousness—being-for-itself—makes impossible *a priori* any eclipse of one thing by another that might prevent the mind seizing and accepting responsibility for a whole dark side of oneself. Sartre may well go on to give Freudianism its due and to suggest an 'existential psychoanalysis', but the net result is to cut off at the roots any possibility of a truly Freudian psychoanalysis.

Freud, then, is accused of having made a number of grave and irreparable mistakes concerning the nature of man, but the objections which assail him from all points of the horizon do not prevent the Freudian doctrine remaining a great and living thing, for a polemic is not carried on with such vehemence against a thing that is dead; psychoanalysis is seen well enough to be an art of treating and curing whose efficacity and value is demonstrated by its many successes. The question, then, is whether Freud's opponents have misunderstood him, or have understood him too well, and whether the danger of psychoanalysis is to man's salvation or to the peace of mind of a few conservative humanists. It is necessary, however, to consider the truth of the Freudian doctrine by means of a direct investigation, and not through the biassed accounts of those who object to it.

The reverse and the obverse of the Freudian theory

Let us risk a summary of all that is original in psychoanalysis: man as conceived by Freud is, in his words as in his actions, a discourse which is ambiguous but decipherable on the supposition of multiple interlocking meanings, both apparent and hidden. Freud as a theorist does not escape from this knot of ambiguity which he has discovered in every man, and his own discourse is equivocal. It is not that it is possible to distinguish in Freud a visible mask and a face which is hidden but clear: things are more mixed up than that, and they cannot be divided as easily into two parts, one artificial and one real; it would be better to say that Freudian doctrine is susceptible of two quite different interpretations, which may even be contradictory, but which are nevertheless consubstantial and go together like the wrong and right sides of the same piece of material.

On one side Freudianism is indistinguishable from a rather insipid scientism which goes back to Freud's years of apprenticeship. If we are to understand materialism in accordance with August Comte's definition as any theory which explains the higher by the lower, for example, mind in terms of the biological and civilization in terms of nature, then Freud is unquestionably materialist; in the name of determinist dogma he relegates free will to the museum of dead metaphysics and, practitioner of a totalitarian medicine, replaces the peripheral categories of moral and immoral by the positive concepts of normal and abnormal; Freud denied the existence of the soul because he could not find it with his psychoanalytic scalpel; he is the proponent of a science which is enemy to the sacred and whose harsh clarity turns the secrets of men's hearts into a popular riddle, or worse, into an obscene charade which melts into nothingness when the answer is discovered. It is as if psychoanalysis were a machine to grind human feeling to dust. In a word, Freud is a desecrator with a triple denial, of mind, morality and mystery.

This is the reverse side of Freudianism, the one usually considered, always refuted because it is refutable, and the most favourable exegesis cannot ignore it or put it in parentheses. But the mistake is usually made of confusing the reverse with the obverse. What is necessary is to put Freud on his feet, as Marx is said to have done with Hegel, because a psychoanalysis which is materialist, amoral and reduced to a prosaic hygiene is literally walking on its head and needs turning the right way up. And so, concepts turn into their contraries, materialism becomes acceptance of the spiritual, to the point of an exaggeration which could be called Cartesian, or rather Bergsonian, denial of morality turns into a dizzy universal moralizing and positivist prose turns in a flash into tragic poetry. It is this reversal of the for and against which gives rise to the ambiguity of the Freudian discourse.

Freud discovered inside man something deep and substantial which could not be of the order of things, of objects, of matter, for man is not man if he is reduced to the narrow and empty consciousness of his body at the present moment. No time is irreparably lost to him: his past history becomes memory, that is to say a basic dimension of his mind. Freud's empirical genius rediscovered this great idea of St Augustine's of memory as man's spiritual depth. This past from which I am separated by the absolute distance constituted by the abyss of irreversibility is nevertheless nearer to me than my body and paradoxically it holds me at the same time as I escape from it. Forgetfulness, for Freud as for Bergson, is an artificial work of repression, useful, defensive or, in extreme cases, an act of bad faith, an apparent ignorance heavy with knowledge, in other words an expression of illusion and falsehood which tries in vain to mask the unity and continuity of human existence. In this context, which must be regarded as one that accepts substance and spirit, Freud's descriptions take on a new note, which is as remarkable as it is unremarked, for example with regard to dreams or to the origins of neurosis. The past watches while the person sleeps and a masked procession of ancient fears and old desires goes by in dreams. A sexual memory from childhood, forgotten in the wrong way, will give rise to and maintain anxiety in adolescence. A materialistic theory would be incapable even of formulating such psychological truths, which are only conceivable if spirit is regarded as a universe in its own right, unbreakable, inviolable.

Freud, then has proved a good witness for human subjectivity against scientism and mechanism, although he spoke their language. Freud's master idea, his Columbus' egg, that simple intuition which it was only necessary to conceive, rests in the hypothesis that mental illnesses have mental causes and that the autonomous science of psychiatry is not the poor relation of neurology. If it is permissible to summarize an immense methodological problem, we may say that the complex from which a person is suffering should be regarded as a psychological obstruction of internal origin, and the psychoanalyst proposes to cure the mind by treating the mind: bodily illness, whether organic or functional, responds to a diagnosis and therapy basically different from a psychiatric diagnosis and therapy, even if in a particular case they are associated in the same clinical picture. It is just as if there were a double truth about man, one for his soul, the other for his body. And how can one help being reminded of Cartesian dualism, which is today so unjustly looked down on, and accused, moreover, of emphasizing the spiritual, a reproach which should equally well be levelled at Freudianism?

Because Freudianism makes the burden of man so heavy for man to carry, because it thinks that nothing which a mind has once lived through can ever be lost, because it wants a man's every word and action and all his behaviour to maintain the charge of multiple meaning, it imports into consciousness a moral atmosphere which is too serious, and which is, if one may say so, foreign to it. Naturalistic ethics advises man to 'leave his past, as a bird leaves his shadow behind when it flies' and in fact if man possessed such an agreeable power of disavowal, his whole life could be a light and gay adventure, the life of play which the Freudian doctrine has shown to be radically impossible: the more I run away from my past for fear of accepting it, the more it pursues me and torments me. Freud professes a philosophy of play which is more in line with Pascal than with Gide and is the exact opposite of amoral. As described by Freud, human consciousness is completely coloured by remorse. When Adam heard God calling him after he had sinned he was afraid and hid himself because he was naked: the psychology of sin contained in this scriptural episode is repeated in the Freudian analyses, which make anxiety and falsehood inseparable both from consciousness of evil and consciousness in itself. Man as described by Freud is terrified at the same time of his desires and of disapproval, as Adam feared both his nakedness and Yahweh, and he never stops dressing them up and deceiving himself by means of constructions, compromises and metaphors, in dream imagery and in the chiaroscuro of his behaviour, as if clothing suppresses the body and darkness gets rid of God. When Freud sets out his philosophy of man the positivist concepts fall apart in his hands and are transformed into moral and religious categories, but the morality is pessimist and the religion is dark and archaic.

And so Freudianism can be turned inside out like a glove, from naturalism to morality. The operation by which Sartre has changed the unconscious into bad faith does not work outside Freud; it develops amid the Freudian ambiguities. The unconscious of the psychoanalysts resembles in the first place a natural force which pushes man by the shoulders from behind and directs him where he does not want to go; but to make the unconscious into a thing in itself, hermetically sealed and opaque, is to make Freudianism unintelligible and psychoanalysis unusable. The dreamer, says Freud, knows the meaning of his dream, but he does not know that he knows, or, rather, he does not wish to know; similarly the person who is mentally ill knows the cause, or rather the reason, for his neurosis and he hides what he knows from himself out of a repugnance which may be voluntary, but not deliberate or considered. Does not Freud continually repeat that the unconscious is the result of repression? Then what is repressed is not the victim of a pathological duality but the author of its own duplicity; if the idea is followed logically to the end, there is bad faith in neurosis, and the conversation between the psychoanalyst and the patient is not so much a purely medical action as the act of bringing two wills face to face, with a view to a solution by means of an admission which is ultimately of the moral and quasi-religious order. Whence the traditional crisis caused by a resistance which is at its height at the moment the secret is about to show itself and the patient is about to be caught in the act of running away from himself. Psychoanalysis would be a spiritual exercise bringing about a conversion from a false conscience to a true conscience, provided truth is regarded as something more than a limiting concept compromised as soon as reached. Freudianism, which on the wrong side looks like an indulgent and easy-going naturalism, changes into a morality of the Jansenist type, for ever forging sovereign weapons against the deception practised so frequently by our human, too human casuistry.

Again, far from suppressing human feeling, Freudian doctrine carries it to a scarcely bearable point of refinement. The sexual life for Freud bears no resemblance to the embarkation for Cythera. It has a tragic character because it is divided between a life instinct and a death instinct, and because, in addition, man has built for himself a civilization which wildly exalts sexuality and at the same time harshly represses it. Consciousness of a sexuality which is incapable of overcoming its own contradictions except by trembling and precarious symbols can be nothing but a continual anxiety permeating and ravaging the whole of human existence. Freud's critics are in the habit of bringing up what they call his pansexualism; Freud does indeed seem to say that man is nothing but sexuality and he is sometimes understood to have exalted an animal instinct into man's tyrannical master. Here again the idea is ambiguous and it could mean just as well, or even better, that sexuality in man is completely human, that it can only exist in a divided and contrary state, tormented and unsatisfied, and that, like Plato's Eros, it has escaped from animal torpor in order to share the restlessness of spirit.

Freudianism is the opposite of an earthbound positivism because it makes man into a moral tragedy which is perhaps insoluble. Conflict is the faith of our interior kingdom; each of our plans provokes an enemy counterplan, the war is too wearing for us to be able to bear it in its nakedness and truth and we seek an illusory peace by covering up with symbols this drama which we cannot cast out of our lives. In every man Freud saw a tragic poet trying to transmute a story of passion, cruelty and death—his own story—with the beauty of a conventional language and a happiness according to etiquette, custom and appearance. This is the kind of tragedy which the ancients thought called out a mixture of fear and pity, that feeling of horror which opens the way to sacred realities. Dare we conclude that there is something sacred in Freud's conception of man?

The pagan greatness of Freud

The imagination of the ancients saw signs from one end of the universe to the other. Everything was full of gods, and the characteristic of gods is always to be talking, but in riddles and in a language with a double meaning which man has to interpret at his peril. Nothing lacks significance and it is necessary to ask the meaning of the fugitive imagery of a dream, the stumbling of a horse or the stammering words of an oracle. This universal symbolism lends itself to a philosophical exegesis and can be explained by the unity and continuity of a cosmos complete without gaps, in which what is near indicates what is afar, where the part bears the mark of the whole and prophecy is usual and natural because it foretells a fate which is the deep truth of the world. A fate which rules over man as well, and which takes the faceless form of Nemesis, who forgets nothing, remits nothing, exactly links extravagance with downfall, and crime with punishment; as Orestes was condemned to punish a crime by a deed which was itself criminal and then to undergo the punishment of madness, and Oedipus was condemned to murder his father and commit incest with his mother, and also to darkness and exile.

It looks as if Freud became enthralled by this ancient vision of the world and projected its dark clarity on to modern man. It is quite a usual thing in the history of ideas for a Jew who does not believe in the values of his ancestors and who has been seduced by the beauty and depths of Greek fables, and by this myth of myths called fate.

Freud in fact affirms as positive what appears to be negative: he affirms the fulness of what appears to be empty, the hidden purpose of what would seem to be a simple mechanism, for example an omitted action, forgetting something, a stereotyped habit. Everything is significant, particularly actions which look like nothing more than the incoherence of a broken automatism; man—like the universe of the ancient myths—cannot stop himself from displaying his secrets in riddles, since 'he who holds his tongue gives himself away with his hands'. Freud denies chance and transforms it into fate at every turn. He also knows Nemesis, who infuses into nature a morality at once clairvoyant and blind: a censured desire is enough to people our sleep with bad dreams; a well-ordered and well-behaved life can suddenly be troubled with a quite unexpected disturbance by some forgotten sexual slip, an initial repugnance to maternity, a fraudulent action committed and safely covered up long ago. Fate can wait patiently for the day of reckoning, but we always have to pay, sometimes with our reason.

Superficially the Freudian theory puts forward a determinist philosophy, but if we go more deeply into it we find a poetry of fate. The first question it puts to us, and also the last, is whether fate, this dangerous idea, is or is not the definitive truth of man.

It should now be possible to put together a few tentative conclusions:

First, to separate Freudianism into a theory which is fundamentally wrong and a practice which is fruitful is a too facile solution to be convincing. Freud could not have been at the same time a faulty theorist and a practician of genius, and this sort of dissociation has something artificial about it and is somewhat divorced from reality. Psychoanalysis carries within itself simple, new and living intuitions, which are of the same order as the theory, even if they are not always explicit. It is difficult to throw Freud out of the window and at the same time welcome him with wide open doors.

Secondly, there is the attractive and well-intentioned attempt to save both Freudian doctrine and psychoanalysis at one blow by discovering in the former a masked acceptance of the spiritual and in the latter a method of conversion to the truth and a moral technique of frank admission; mental illness would be a flight into a universe of idols, and constructions like those of dreams would be explained by a lowering of spiritual energy. But it is still necessary to ask whether the Freudian conception of man does not need a rather drastic revision, whether its tragic emphasis does not lead to a radical pessimism, ceding too much to fate and not enough to liberty.

Thirdly, Freudian doctrine has a clear dialectical value in so far as it serves to unmask and contest a number of ideologies which, in fact, dissolve at its contact: traditional pedestrian psychologies of an academic intellectualism which scorns to look at what there really is in man; positivist sociology and Marxist historicism, neither of which can allow the individual man any personal adventure or private drama; existentialism, which refuses all content to consciousness and throws man outside himself on to the highways of the world. Freudian doctrine reminds these ideologies quite sharply that man not only has a fate, but that he is fate and that he weighs out for himself a weight which no objective balance can measure.

It is undeniable that the Freudian doctrine has rediscovered the equivocal attitude of man without God. To say everything in such an easy formula is also to say nothing. The treatise on how good use can be made both of the theory and of the practice of the Freudian doctrine still remains to be written.